A Western Way of Meditation

A Western Way of Meditation

The Rosary Revisited

David Burton Bryan

A Campion Book

Loyola University Press
Chicago

Printed in the United States of America
♾

Loyola University Press
3441 North Ashland Avenue
Chicago, Illinois 60657

Cover design by Pat Olson

Library of Congress Cataloging-in-Publication Data

Bryan, David Burton.
A Western way of meditation : the rosary revisited / by David Burton Bryan.
p.
Includes bibliographical references and index.
ISBN 0-8294-0715-4 (paper)
ISBN 0-8294-0727-8 (cloth)
1. Rosary. 2. Meditation—Catholic Church. 3. Catholic Church—Prayer-books and devotions—English. I. Title.
BX2163.B73 1991
242'.74—dc20 91-14245
CIP

Contents

Foreword

Among Catholic Christians the rosary is still a familiar prayer, though not as familiar nor as widely practiced as in the recent past. As an Irish Dominican, I am, on two counts, acutely conscious of the situation. Dominican tradition has it that the rosary was revealed, by Our Lady, to Dominic. Unhappily, hard-nosed historians have put paid to that story! The fact remains that the rosary has been fostered and promulgated by the Order, but much less so than formerly. In the bitterest days of religious persecution, when Mass was unavailable, the rosary was the fallback of Irish Catholics and a foremost means of sustaining them in the faith. In my youth the family rosary—a chaplet recited by the family at evening—was a regular practice in Irish homes. No more. I am not suggesting that the rosary ever was a Dominican or Irish preserve; it was, and is, a quite popular prayer in North America and worldwide as well. I only seek to document, from personal experience, a decline in the use of the rosary. Decline—by no means extinction.

There must, however, be reason for the decline. A main reason is that the rosary is misunderstood and undervalued. Superficially it does look like a prayer fit only for the unlettered—for the "simple faithful" whose simple faith it will leave benignly undisturbed. The seemingly mindless repetition of *Aves* lends substance to this assessment. And the term *mysteries* can be baffling. Added to this, most writing on the rosary, usually in the form of leaflets and pious booklets, is calculated to repel anyone in search of a sound way of prayer. The rosary deserves better, very much better.

David Burton Bryan, as an academic and, patently, as a *pray-er* of the rosary, has charted that better way. He has discerned and uncovered the very heart of the rosary: it is a venerable and sophisticated prayer of meditation. It is also extraordinarily rich.

Bryan's approach is at once conventional and unconventional. In the first place, he shows the rosary to be a thoroughly biblical prayer. After all, but for the last two of the fifteen mysteries, all are straight from the Gospels, predominantly from Luke. A prayer that demands serious meditation on the announcement of the coming of Jesus, on his birth, his passion and death, on his resurrection and ascension, has to be an essentially Christian prayer. In this book, which is meant to introduce people to the riches of the rosary, we find a first look at the fifteen mysteries and, then, a consideration at greater depth. Sound pedagogy, yes, but also food for veteran rosary meditators.

As for the prayers, the author stresses the importance of all three: Our Father, Hail Mary, and Glory. He insists that they should be *prayed* slowly and meditatively; he highlights the primacy of the Our Father. And he links the rosary with the Eucharist and the Liturgy of the Hours. A link, but not in any sense a substitute for one or the other.

More unconventional, but remarkably enlightening, are some of Bryan's other points. He observes that while in practice the rosary is a Catholic prayer, it might well, as a basic way of meditation, have an appeal not only beyond Catholic but even beyond Christian circles. He sets the rosary, firmly, in a long tradition of meditation. And, for those who find the repetitious Hail Marys offputting, he has the salutary reminder of the place of repetition in religion and meditation.

Notably suggestive is Bryan's association of the rosary with what he calls the *baqqesh* tradition, a Judeo-Christian-Islamic way of meditation. *Baqqesh,* a key term in the book, is a Hebrew word meaning "seek" or "search." Bryan uses it as a portmanteau word to include also awaiting, watching, hoping. He casts Mary as the great Listener, *the* person to whom we can praise God and her Son, and as the Patron or Sponsor who stands beside us and encourages us to pray. Indeed, he sketches a very satisfying mariology. And, perhaps unexpectedly, we have a fascinating presentation of the Trinity. In short, a main strength of the book is its solid theology. All the while there is the practical dimension: step-by-step suggestions. The author passionately desires his readers to learn to appreciate, to come to love, and, above all, to *pray* the rosary.

David Burton Bryan has not written "another" book on the rosary. He has written what is, quite simply, the best book available. I, for one, find myself after a lifetime of rosary prayer—perhaps, sadly, not always rosary-meditation!—introduced to a deeper and richer appreciation of it. This is a book that will make its mark. It is an honor, and a pleasure, to contribute this foreword.

Wilfrid J. Harrington, O.P.

Introduction

The English-speaking nations, for twenty-five years now, have been showing an uncharacteristic interest in meditation. The evidence can be seen at the corner bookstore: all the great cultural and religious traditions of the world have supplied their honored methods. Perhaps we should not wonder. Meditation lies at the core of the human spirit, and even busy America would not ignore it forever.

Missing at the corner bookstore are books on the rosary. This is surprising, since the rosary is clearly the world's single most popular form of meditation. No doubt the larger public avoids the rosary because it thinks it a purely Catholic thing (this book challenges that assumption). But rosary meditators themselves do not analyze their art; much less do they wonder at the little notice it receives in books.

To millions who do not know the rosary personally, it seems to be only the childlike prattling of a prayer called the "Hail Mary," which drones from the AM radio on evenings in October or May. That blur of sound, some people notice, is interrupted after every tenth Hail Mary by the more widely known prayer of Christ, the "Our Father." A few people may even have been told that rosary users are all the while meditating with the help of the "mysteries," scenes from the four Gospels that stimulate meditative powers. But how many guess that the rosary ranks among humanity's great paths of meditation? Do rosary users themselves know it? (For a chart showing the outward form of the rosary and its accompanying beads, see page xviii.)

Thomas Merton, America's best known meditator and monk, was a pilgrim to Tibet. Merton knew that, if meditation becomes an American habit, our thanks will go chiefly to the Far East. Hinduism, Buddhism, Taoism, and the others have intrigued us and have alerted us to our ignorance of other cultures. More to the point, they have renewed our interest in meditation.

Science, too, has cautiously entered the field. A recent spate of books seeks to demonstrate that, at the frontiers of physics, the analytical methods of traditional science have limitations that can best be overcome by the more intuitive and holistic approaches of meditation as practiced in the East. Fritjof Capra's *The Tao of Physics* was a pioneer in this effort, and he has received much encouragement from other physicists.[1] At the same time, anthropologists have been assuring us that people of the nonindustrialized world see things that we no longer glimpse. The "Don Juan" books of Carlos Castaneda, those fictional compendia of pop anthropology, sent a generation hankering after the perceptual life of native Americans.

The discovery of the meditative strengths of preindustrial and non-Western humanity can only be welcomed. So exciting are the possible benefits for Western civilization that one hesitates to complain that our own meditative traditions, now admittedly frail, are being overlooked. But there are tender shoots on our own ancient roots, and some of us, myself included, have a strong preservationist instinct. We will water any sprout, no matter how desperate its condition. Thus Elie Wiesel is vigorously watering the roots of Hasidic Judaism, while Christian enthusiasts are issuing new editions of medieval Christian classics such as *The Cloud of Unknowing* and the *Revelations of Divine Love* of Juliana of Norwich. The rosary, clearly, is such a tender Western plant.

The lingering prominence of the rosary cannot be doubted. Leaflets by the hundreds of thousands are sold annually among us at little more than cost. To these we may add a number of booklets, usually in small editions, bequeathing us the fruit of their authors' rosary meditations. New catechisms typically print

---

[1] Revised edition, New York: Bantam Books, 1984.

a diagram of the rosary, and general books on meditation often pay the rosary homage.

But even here one finds signs that the ancient plant needs watering. The hundreds of thousands of leaflets sold annually are mostly reprints, and are, in any case, quite unhelpful. The booklets giving the fruit of rosary meditations, some by prominent prelates, are too often marred by biblical fundamentalism and mere sentimentality; in few cases do they give us much hope for our personal, nonderivative, meditation. Diagrams in catechisms, such as the one on page xviii, are nearly useless by themselves. And general books on meditation give the rosary homage only: the authors seldom think it worth their trouble to investigate the rosary, to link it to their own theories of meditation. Finally, full-length books about the rosary are extremely rare, and almost nonexistent are rosary books that make use of recent advances in human knowledge. Even the achievements of modern biblical studies have seldom been employed.[2] Though the rosary is still a large plant, it shows many signs of needing cultivation. It needs to be revisited.

What is wrong? Our rosary tradition undoubtedly suffers from every malaise that has attached itself to Western civilization. The rape of the environment weakens our natural perception of the sacred. Tranquility is made difficult by the hectic pace of mindless change. Spectator entertainment renders our spirits passive. We put a price tag on everything and then wonder why our vision is no longer poetic. World hunger, even genocide, desensitizes us.

But many who deplore these factors remain uninterested in the rosary. A second retinue of reasons must be marshaled to explain the situation. The rosary is a way of meditation based on prayer, an activity that many moderns have come to distrust. The rosary, too, developed in a framework of Catholic doctrines once generally accepted in Western civilization. Some of these, obviously, are no longer widely held outside the Catholic Church. In some quarters, too, the rosary is not considered respectable; it con-

---

[2] A highly recommendable exception is Wilfrid J. Harrington, O.P., *The Rosary: A Gospel Prayer* (New York: Alba House, 1975).

jures up images of elderly immigrants, shepherd children, and nineteenth-century art, often cluttered with easy sentimentality and roses in profusion. Amazingly, the rosary tradition is not supported by special schools and seminars, or, as I have said, by numerous books. Its advocates, seemingly, share few secrets among themselves; much less do they attempt to popularize their methods. The rosary has no gurus. Finally, it suffers from being ours. It is not exotic. We will all believe that there is special knowledge among the tribes of the vanishing rain forests or on the slopes of the Himalayas. Claims closer to home are cynically (and sometimes with reason) dismissed.

I have spent my life among academics. The prevailing view in my circle has been that the rosary cannot speak to the sophistication of the scholarly mind. To me, this idea is rubbish. The real problem for us academics was isolated by Capra and, of course, many before him: we have placed our world of concepts (fascinating and useful as it is) so firmly in front of all reality that we can no longer deal with life directly.

If this were only a problem for academics, civilization could draw a sigh of relief, for academics are a minority of the people. But two factors prevent such an easy escape. First, academic concepts are increasingly a playground for all. The inhibitions of professors now attack everyone. Second, the divorce between the rosary and academics hurts both sides, for academics bring tradition and new discoveries together.

My remarks about the failure of rosary books to incorporate modern studies, even biblical studies, may lead one to expect a scholarly book. I have indeed striven to make use of the discoveries of the scholars in a number of areas. Practitioners of these sciences will recognize some familiar ground. But I have not provided my book with numerous notes or credits. I have not attempted to give exhaustive justification for my choice of modern insights. The book aims at something more practical. It is not only the world of scholarship that has not yet been connected to rosary writings. Even a thoroughgoing "how-to" book, of the sort for which America is famous, has not yet appeared. Such practical guides as have been published are, in my view, either too short, too lacking in modern discoveries, or, sometimes, simply wrong about rosary meditation. While my own book will undoubtedly be thought wrong by some, only actual rosary users, old or new, can be its judges.

Fritjof Capra and others have described Eastern meditation as leading to a perception of reality that is organic, unitive, and intuitive. An elaborate demonstration that rosary meditation achieves the same ends has yet to be made. Also yet to be written is a full-length study of the rosary's "mysteries" from the point of view of modern biblical studies (enlarging on Wilfrid Harrington's study), including the development of rosary themes in the course of later Christian history. While these larger projects are tempting, I have here pursued them only to the extent demanded by a practical introduction to the rosary. For it seemed more important for us rosary meditators to water our own plant before writing full-length studies of it.

Rosary meditation is really a mix of several ancient techniques (see page 27), all of which have pre-Christian, even prehistoric, antecedents. During most of the long history of Christianity, those who sought to pursue an inner life (and they were legion) discovered their own mixes of meditational elements. Hermits, monks, nuns, as well as contemplative people in everyday life, all recognized that their journeys were their own. Even a monastery supplied mainly logistic supports. Though large numbers avidly pursued the inner life, and many met success, meditation had never been analyzed or even, in fact, named.

Then, rather suddenly toward the end of the Middle Ages, one particular mix evolved rapidly and established itself under the name of the *rosarium* ("rose garden"). The rosary did not achieve a radically new blend of meditational elements; its novelty lay mainly in the fact that it could be easily taught and rapidly disseminated. Within two centuries, mainly through the efforts of the Order of Preachers ("Dominicans"), it spread throughout Europe, giving all who wished it an open door to the meditative traditions of the West, albeit in a single form. Yet no one then analyzed the achievement of the rosary. It was, and often still is, thought to be merely an exceptional instrument of devotion.

As such, the rosary is still eminently teachable, and thus deserves to be the subject of books. The difficulties today lie not so much with the rosary as with the general decline of the poetic and contemplative spirit. This book claims little new except the application of modern discoveries and remedies for modern difficulties.

Since the rosary's creators did not analyze the rosary for us, can the reader be confident that this book is not merely the author's private system? In my opinion there is a consistency in rosary meditation from person to person and from century to century. If I am right, then nearly any rosary book based, as this one is, on real meditation would arrive at many of the same conclusions. But am I right? In the present state of our rosary art, I doubt if there is enough data to permit me to prove my contention. Many more rosary meditators must write books!

Meanwhile, in my own book, I tentatively—even fearfully—begin to add to the rosary's ancient soil a mix of modern discoveries in biblical studies, primitive anthropology, spirituality, and theology. Some will doubtless find my sprinklings of science (which has been for me no more than a lifelong avocation) less essential. My intent here is to introduce a certain suggestiveness to my material. The rosary does deal with mysteries, and science very recently has learned to stand at the brink and gaze along with the rest of us.

✣ ✣ ✣

My first rosary was put in my hands when I was nine years old. I remember the day well, for it was the day of my baptism, and the donor was Father John E. Doherty, C. Ss. R. I am grateful to him for that, and because he has always remained a practitioner. To Father Wilfrid Harrington, O.P., I tender heartfelt thanks for his support and for his generous foreword. Thanks also are due to my sister-in-law, Melissa Lee Bryan, who entered on disk the first version of this book, and to the many who have given encouragement, especially to Sister Marion Chaloux, R.H.S.J., to my mother, Jeanne Bryan, to my brother Frank, to my sister Jane, and to my wife, Jean. And in Vermont, high on the flanks of Couching Lion, live Carl and Mary Zeno, who know the odor of the roses; to them I dedicate this book.

The Pattern of the Rosary

The diagram of the rosary, as given below, is essential to the beginner, yet it can lead to misunderstandings concerning rosary meditation. Read chapter 1, "Basic Ideas about the Rosary."

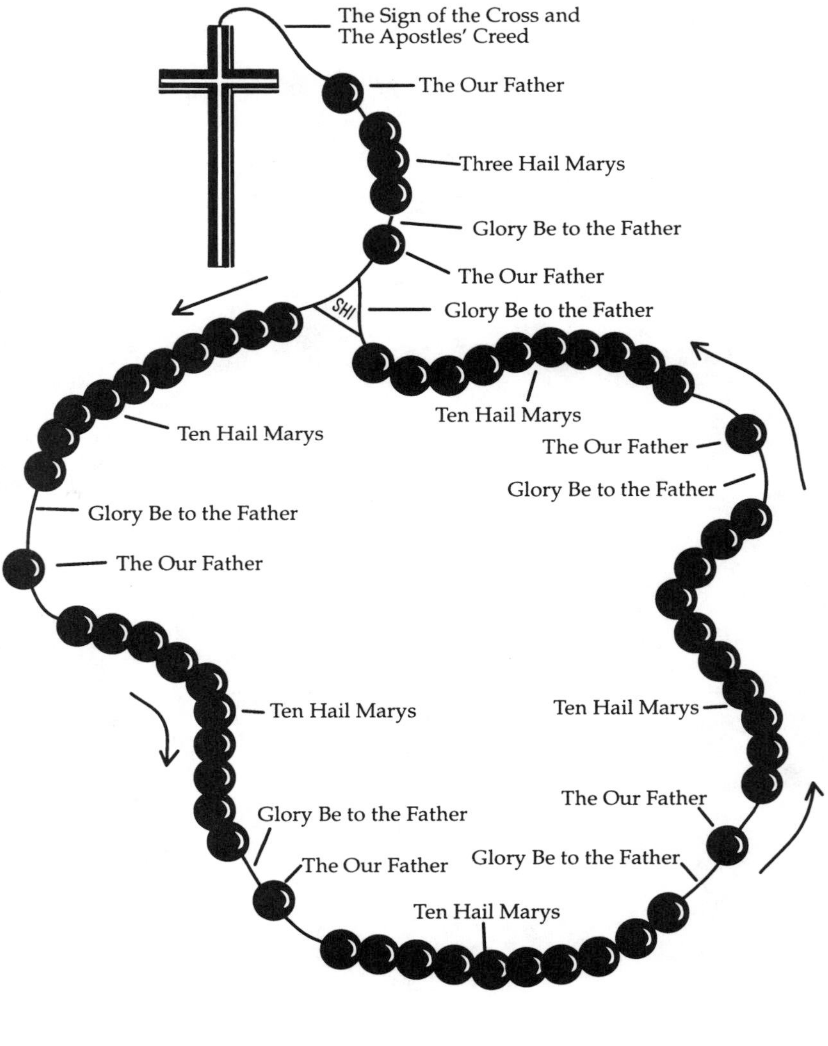

Texts of the Rosary Prayers

[for the Apostles' Creed, see page 159]

Sign of the Cross:

In the Name of the Father, and of the Son, and of the Holy Spirit. Amen.

The Our Father:

Our Father who art in heaven, hallowed by thy Name. Thy Kingdom come, thy will be done, on earth as it is in heaven. Give us this day our daily bread, and forgive us our trespasses as we forgive those who trespass against us. Lead us not into temptation, but deliver us from evil. Amen.

The Hail Mary:

Hail Mary, full of grace, the Lord is with thee. Blessed art thou among women and blessed is the fruit of thy womb, Jesus. Holy Mary, Mother of God, pray for us sinners now and at the hour of our death. Amen.

The "Glory Be" (Doxology):

Glory be to the Father, and to the Son, and to the Holy Spirit, as it was in the beginning, is now, and ever shall be, world without end. Amen.

1

Basic Ideas about the Rosary

Standing at the rose gate, the reader, perhaps, has decided to enter the famous path, now comparatively quiet, that is still the world's best known way of meditation. It may be frustrating, then, to discover that the first bead on the rosary is not reached until page 50.

But the work of the meditator begins here. These introductory chapters take us first into a fore-garden that turns out to be our own. Our task is to take pencil and paper and, with the help of chapters 1 and 2, make a survey, or at least a few notes, concerning what we find within ourselves.

If a monk of Mount Sinai asked that we visit our inner selves before ascending the path that Moses, thirty-three centuries ago, took up into the fiery cloud, we would hasten to comply. (The rosary, in fact, does incorporate Moses' path.) We are not, in any case, mere tourists on this journey. We are discoverers. When we are well into our adventure we will be glad to have made an inner inventory while we were still at home.

1. Prayer

In any method of meditation there is always something one *does* or, at least allows to happen, in one's innermost self. One method begins with the attempt to think of nothing. Another begins with the attempt to give fullest attention to something, an object, perhaps, or a task.

Rosary meditation begins with the act of greeting. It is as simple, and as difficult, as saying "hello." Greeting is surely among the most basic human powers and is of the essence of communication, yet we are usually content to deliver a cheap imitation.

Sometimes a person, utterly alone, will launch a greeting into the limitless unknown. To do so is to claim kinship with reality as a whole and to its full depth, to assert communion with Being as such. But the greeting in the void also expresses our absolute right to be recognized as individuals.

In our Western tradition we credit unity to the invisible partner of such speech, calling that partner "God." As part of our overzealous program for subdividing all reality, we have a special word for this sort of communication: we call it prayer. But the larger and more basic word remains "communication." The rosary, then, is a method of meditation built on prayer or, speaking less precisely, on the act of communication.

It is exactly here that some of our contemporaries may find the rosary initially unattractive: we are already talking about "God" as if we were experts, like so many middle managers who brag about getting memos through to the Chief Executive Officer. Should we not be more sensitive to the fact that "God" means different things to different people, that there are many different experiences of God? Ought we pretend to such familiarity with our partner in mystery?

The complaint has some merit; many praying people make God seem like an old uncle living with the family, someone so familiar as to be practically invisible until we want him for something. Prayer often trivializes the "limitless unknown." But let the new meditator be assured that rosary meditation, correctly practiced, is aware of the great mystery denoted by the term *God*. When I discuss prayer, I do so cautiously, leaving plenty of room for *all* experiences of the divine.

A traditional Western definition is properly cautious: prayer is the "raising of the heart and mind to God."[3] God, in this definition, signifies the Creator, the heavenly Father, or, if we prefer, the Supreme Being. For others, the word may equally well signify the Great Spirit, the Ground of Being, or the Totally Other. When we say that we "raise the mind and heart," we mean that we thrust our intelligence (mind) and will (heart) toward the Unknown. We deliberately move our loose, many-faceted, and tentative selves toward the One, the Self-Possessed. To use the more accustomed words, we move our created selves toward the Uncreated Creator. In reality, as we will discover, the main work of bringing Creator and created into contact (communication) is done by the Creator. Our "raising of mind and heart" is largely a matter of removing the obstacles to God's approach. The basic game in the universe turns out to be communication, and we are not, after all, alone.

[In this book I lean heavily on traditional language, while frequently returning to the fact of the limitless unknown. It should be noted that calling God "Father" and "he" does not imply that God is a male. All the highest human qualities, in whichever sex they may be found, are needed for our poor attempt to form a distant idea of God. Similarly the reader should note that reference to the Church as "she" does not imply that the Church is female. The use of gender specific terms should be thought of as metaphorical, and therefore limited, rather than literal.]

It is amazing that Western civilization's most famous definition of prayer is so little known in the West. Many people, whatever the extent of their educations, think that prayer is little more than asking God for things. This impoverished notion is undoubtedly fostered by the many Christians who pray only when they want something!

---

[3] This definition, best known from the eighth-century Orthodox theologian John Damascene, is considered basic in both the Greek and Latin churches.

Johann Metz offers a definition of prayer that effectively combines "mind and heart" from the traditional definition: "To pray is to say Yes to God" against the background of the troubles and sufferings of life. And because our "yes" is said amid all the forces of modern life, which are combining to render us anonymous, prayer is still "the oldest form of the human battle for subjectivity and identity against all odds."[4]

Scientists are now beaming intelligible messages out into the universe in the hope that life in other worlds may hear us and answer. Prayer is similar, except that it takes God's existence as actual and not merely possible. Prayer assumes that he is conscious of our attempts and treats our communications seriously, provided that our messages are sincere, that the voices we use are really ours.

Asking God for favors is, of course, one way to raise one's heart and mind to God, as our definition requires. But prayer itself does not consist in the asking, but rather in the raising.

The first step in rosary meditation is the greeting in the limitless unknown. If you are lucky enough to live where the sky is free of light pollution, perhaps you will go out under the stars. An empty house may serve as well, or one may try shouting silently inward, through the gaps in one's own being. But this should not be a grim exercise; recall that each of us exists and has a voice whose use, as in childhood, we can enjoy. What words you choose, if any, are completely your decision.

2. How Does Prayer Work?

It is useless to argue about prayer with one who will not try it. Prayer is like a new diet or a new kind of furniture polish: the proof of the product depends on testing it. Prayer *works*, which does not mean that it is a method of getting one's wishes granted.

---

[4] Johann Metz and Karl Rahner, *The Courage to Pray* (Crossroad: New York, 1981; original, *Ermutigung zum Gebet*, 1977) 11, 24.

If prayer does not enable us to have our way with God, to tame the Unknown, then how do we know that it is having an effect? Again, talk is of little avail, but actual trial may produce results that one can recognize as prayer's effect. Many words have been used to describe the results of prayer, words such as "joy," "personal growth," "peace," "new life," and so forth. But none of these words actually conveys the unique quality of the results of prayer. God, if I may speak mythologically, has his own touch, a sort of gentleness and certitude combined. But it further seems that God, the Master Communicator, has a special touch for each of us: he speaks through a unique language of events that fits the sort of person into which we are developing. A praying person learns to recognize (occasionally!) the touch of God. It is something that cannot be ascertained in advance by consulting experts or their books, this one included.

Returning to the simplicity of our starting point, prayer is communication. It brings speaker and Speaker into union. I must add an element to the idea of "raising the mind and heart": the Creator also seeks this union.

We have all met people, often newly "converted," who think they get constant messages, all as clear as telegrams, from God. Perhaps some do, but in rosary meditation we assume that we will need time to *learn* (relearn?) to be sensitive to prayer's divine response. God may speak with the voices of cataracts and thunderclaps, but we have long since made ourselves deaf.

From this point the reader should take care to remember daily events. Because the invention of writing has vastly weakened our memories, most of us now have no choice but to commit events to paper.

3. Nonverbal Prayer

Since speech is one of the most distinctive features of the human species, we need not apologize for the fact that rosary meditation begins with verbal speech, verbal prayer. As communication develops, however, nonverbal union is certainly a possibility, even an expectation. Ultimately one hopes one's speech becomes as if it were divine: a language of events. Our words, in that case, become deeds, and our deeds become our words. Like God's event-words, ours will even have a certain creative effect. Thus the rosary, like other systems of meditation worldwide, reaches out into the *doing* and the *being* of its practitioners, guiding them into wholeness.

4. Prayer of Petition

From what has been said, should we conclude that we are never to cry out to God for help? Certainly not. He is the Creator, the Unifier, the Giver, and we raise our being toward him when we acknowledge this fact by expressing our needs as we see them. But it is the *style* of God's answer which should particularly interest us, not the blunt fact of whether this or that concern of ours is resolved. If we try to notice the style of this event-speech, we will come to know how to recognize that God is giving *himself*, a better communication than any particular benefit he might confer. Additionally, it is well to recall that often we do not pray with much sincerity. Once our prayer is "granted," we are the first to wish it had not been heard! We repudiate the unforeseen consequences of that for which we asked. We have, in any case, little idea of what is best for us.[5]

5. Prayer and Meditation

Meditation may be defined as a way of tapping the tremendous resources of our minds and wills for the purpose of giving us a new and deeper contact with reality. Methods of meditation,

---

[5] Many moderns, including Catholics, are still trapped in the dilemma proposed two centuries ago by the deists: a God who would change his supposedly perfect plans at our request would be no God. But there are no time sequences in the Creator; we and our requests have always been present in his "now." Any changes are only in our world of change.

then, need not be built upon the specific elements of religion (prayers to God, holy pictures, and the like), a point often made by advocates of certain Eastern ways of meditation. Indeed, many individuals have developed methods of meditation based simply on their own contacts with daily life: physicists, poets, musicians, psychologists, farmers, and homemakers have done as much.

Some of the powers of mind and will that respond to meditation are the familiar powers of memory, attentiveness, concentration, and endurance. Less obvious, but more important in the long run, are our powers of openness, of "letting be," of listening, acceptance, and intuition. And there are powers deep within us that correspond to the familiar "religious" terms of faith, hope, and love. These three must be involved if we are to contact reality as it truly is in itself.

A system of meditation based on prayer, as is the rosary, employs a special meditative device: by asking us to pray, it asks us to raise our minds and hearts, centering their powers on a point, which is the *person* to whom we pray. Although it is possible to center our powers on practically anything (ourselves, for example, or an imaginary point, or the petal of an apple blossom), the rosary's method of directing our energies to another person has much to recommend it. Persons, we know, have power to touch our resources. In the presence of a person certain areas of our knowing and willing faculties come alive.

In prayer, of course, the "person" on whom we chiefly focus is God. In order that this sort of meditation be most effective, it is obviously necessary to avoid certain negative notions and feelings concerning God. According to the teachings of Jesus Christ, we ought to view God not only as our Creator and Master, but also as our loving parent. A good parent, while motivated by great love for his or her child, also teaches the child to respect the parent's freedom and rights. This awareness of God's love and freedom (both!) will, as Jesus showed, speedily unlock the heavy door of separation that often prevents communication between creature and Creator. The parent-child symbol, according to Johann Metz, brings to meditation certain valuable assets from childhood: the confidence we once knew, but also the longing and questioning.[6] The confidence of prayer is thus not an "artificial or dubious naïveté" but rather a "spontaneous existential optimism."

A further impetus to communication with God can be discerned in the person of Jesus Christ himself. Our meditation does not require that we deny our own human nature, attempting to become some sort of disembodied spirits. Instead we are given a human model, Jesus, to keep before our eyes. We are told that fidelity to this human model will give us a ready key to union with God. Finally, as is well known, the rosary places before us the person of Mary, the mother of Jesus, whose life, a portrait of the ideal disciple of Jesus, stirs many of the powers within us.

The mere mention of the names *Father, Jesus,* and *Mary* thus puts us at the beginning of a natural and universal track leading us ever deeper into the real. But the rosary goes further by leading us through fifteen famous scenes (called "mysteries") in the life of Christ. These scenes span the whole course of a human life, beginning before birth and extending past the moment of death (see number 30). In this way, they touch us at key moments in our own lives and in the lives of those around us.

Although, as has been said, meditation certainly need not take religion as its starting point, rosary meditation does have the advantage of energizing meditation through *divine* communication. Perhaps this is true, less explicitly, in all systems, since all aim at a deeper contact with fundamental reality.

From what has just been said it might seem that the rosary is full of detail and complexity, preventing the focusing of our minds and hearts. In reality the opposite is true. The details of the prayers and mysteries become part of the furniture of our minds. Far from drawing attention to themselves, they concentrate our natural powers on the persons we address and, uniquely, on the God whom we greet.

---

[6] Metz and Rahner, *The Courage to Pray,* op cit., 24.

6. Hope, Prayer, and the Prayer of Petition

The more we meditate with prayer as our foundation, the more our idea of God (however framed) is purified of unhelpful conceptions. We come increasingly to appreciate the great good will that God has for all his creatures. Conversely, the better our idea of God becomes, the more effective is our prayer and our meditation.

God, we may imagine, has almost unlimited blessings stored up for us; his beneficence can be limited only by *our* weaknesses, our insincerity, and our unwillingness to accept the consequences of our communication with him. God, it seems, knows his gifts would be wasted by those who do not really understand or appreciate them. Many blessings are kept in storage, as it were, awaiting the existence of some person who understands and really desires them. Our word for this enlightened form of desire is *hope*. Perhaps, as Anthony Bloom taught, elaborating on the gospel story of blind Bartimaeus, a person who has sunk to despair is often the one who can hope with sufficient intensity.[7]

A person animated by an increasingly pure hope gradually learns to want exactly those things that God really wants to give. In such a person, the prayer of petition is not self-centered; it is a sort of high union with the divine mind that gives God a person to whom he can entrust benefits long predetermined. Thus pivotal improvements in human history are associated with persons whose motives and attitudes were exceptionally divine. Meditation of all kinds, and perhaps especially meditation based on prayer, affects not only ourselves but, increasingly, those around us.

7. *Baqqesh:* A Judeo-Christian-Islamic Way of Meditation

The traditions of the Bible (both Testaments) give hints of a rich variety of meditative methods. Rosary meditation has its origins

---

[7] Anthony Bloom, *Beginning to Pray* (New York: Paulist Press, 1982), 71–73.

in the ancient Near East (the world of the Bible) and, in particular, in those meditative traditions that we may call the method of *baqqesh* (pronounced "bakkaysh").

The peoples of the ancient Near East were not highly analytical; certainly they never developed our modern concern for using one precisely defined word for each thing that comes up in a serious discussion. Thus, instead of having one word for meditation, the ancient Jews and Jewish Christians favored a whole series of overlapping terms that, taken together, rounded out their ideas of meditation. One such series of terms included words meaning "seek," "search," "await," "expect," "watch," "hope," and even "petition." In this book I have selected the first of these words ("seek," Hebrew: *baqqesh*) to stand for all the rest.

I have already referred (on the preceding page) to the power of hope: a person who has a deep, unselfish, and enlightened hope for something God has already planned will make it possible for God to carry out his plan. Thus, when the Bible speaks of seeking, searching, awaiting, or hoping for God, it refers to seek-ing the development of some divine (real) plan. The unfolding of these plans gives us an ever-improving idea of who or what God is, thus intensifying the power of our meditation (which is directed to God as to a person). Simultaneously, God's language of events becomes clarified for us. It is no accident that the biblical writer who speaks most often of "seeking" is Luke, and from Luke we get most of the mysteries of the rosary. These scenes from the life of Christ are dramatizations of the act of seeking.

The idea that we can hasten divine plans by our mere seeking (*baqqesh*) may seem childish, even superstitious. But it is exactly here that the closest parallels with modern physics are seen. For quantum physics shows that realities may exist at *various* coordinates in space-time (some of which would be "future" to us) and, further, that the shapes of these still undiscovered realities are related to our own investigative methods, our own *baqqesh* (see also number 31). Human beings, the Destroyers, can, if they will, be junior partners in creation.

The idea of *baqqesh* includes the complimentary idea of "awaiting" (Hebrew: *qawweh*).[8] Rosary meditators soon learn that they do not merely invent rich inner lives for themselves as writers may do. Much of meditation, rather, consists in becoming open to reality, waiting for reality to reveal itself. In this sense, rosary meditation is similar to what is traditionally called "contemplation" (see numbers 13 and 49).

"Waiting" has always been a part of Western spirituality, at least from the time when our ancestors began to describe themselves as servants of their respective gods. The term *Waiting* is partially equivalent to what is called "remaining in the presence of God," "the prayer of simple regard,"[9] or even "experiencing the absence of God."[10]

It may be said that the inner method of rosary meditation is *Greeting* (the opening of communication), preceded or followed by *Waiting* in the silence (darkness) before the Other, a waiting in which a certain *Seeking* already begins. One is searching for any signs of the Kingdom, signs of hope fulfilled.

Greeting/Waiting/Seeking—all parts of the basic act of communication—may just as well serve as a valuable meditative technique quite apart from prayer. One might thus approach another person or even a stone or an imaginary Void. But it comes most fully into its own when conducted in the presence of the Father.

Baqqesh, it may be noted, is what Jesus sometimes called "knocking on the door" (Luke 11:9), an image for prayer used effectively by Anthony Bloom and many others.[11]

---

[8] See Bernard Häring's beautiful chapter "The Prayer of Vigilance," pages 101–13 in his *Prayer: The Integration of Faith and Life* (Notre Dame, Ind.: Fides Publishers, 1975). An eloquent Islamic prayer of *baqqesh* is given on page 3.

[9] See Bernard Basset, *Let's Start Praying Again* (Garden City, N.Y.: Doubleday/Image, 1973) pages 103, 104; also John Catoir, *Enjoy the Lord: A Path to Contemplation* (New York: The Christophers, 1978) pages 85–94; and George A. Maloney, *Alone with the Alone* (Notre Dame, Ind.: Ave Maria Press, 1982) pages 1–28.

[10] See Anthony Bloom, *Beginning to Pray,* op. cit., pages 25–36; and because God remains the totally other, one waits without being able to see, a fact central to chapters 3–8 of the medieval *The Cloud of Unknowing* (James Walsh, ed., Ramsey, N.J.: Paulist, 1981) pages 119–39.

[11] *Beginning to Pray,* op. cit., pages 71, 72.

8. Asceticism and the Rosary

Meditators from all previous centuries and all world traditions would find a glaring omission in this book: its lack of elaborate ascetical advice. All systems of meditation, whether of the Far East or in the Judeo-Christian-Islamic tradition, have insisted that success in meditation rests on a serious struggle against our moral defects and even against anything whatsoever that limits the interior liberty of the meditator.

It was taken for granted by our ancestors that all forms of deliberate injustice on the part of the meditator would make meditation impossible. Further, intemperance in the use of food, drink, ease, sleep, comforts, sex, entertainments, or anything at all was seen as preventing progress in meditation. Equally limiting were obsessive human relationships as well as interior illusions generated by faulty self-estimates. Even excessive attachment to legitimate goods and wholesome things, such as family love, land, and public office, were seen as making meditation difficult, and the final plunge into Reality would require one to cease entirely the habit of keeping an eye on oneself in the approaching prospect of union.

The rigor of the ascetical struggle outlined above has usually led to the founding of monasteries, a solution whose necessity is being challenged in modern times. One might say that an asceticism of life *in* the world has been developing for the past several centuries, though it is far from clear what form(s) it will finally take. And while in the past there were many approaches (witness the different religious orders in Catholicism), in today's world meditators must examine a much greater variety of approaches to morality and asceticism, most of them more or less untested.

Discouraging as all this may seem, rosary meditation will begin to guide our search for forms of asceticism best for us. Doubtless all meditators agree that meditation and life grow together[12] or

---

[12] On the interaction of life-issues and meditation, Anthony Bloom's *Beginning to Pray* is highly recommended. His experiences as an emigré from Russia, a member of the French underground, and a physician as well as a monk, evoke the seriousness of the impassioned meditators of former times.

they do not grow at all. And a system based on prayer, perhaps more than any other, is clearly impossible if the meditator is determined to live an unexamined life.

Living guides ("spiritual directors") for the ascetical project are important but notoriously difficult to find. There are undoubtedly exemplary ascetics in every walk of life, persons who have learned to use ordinary events and duties as the whetstones of their ascetical efforts. Unfortunately, in modern Catholicism at least, there is little effort made to locate and empower such experienced guides.

For many centuries, Catholics were encouraged to seek spiritual direction in the confessional, but the assumption that the two needs (spiritual direction and reconciliation) should be so tightly linked is justly questioned today. In any case, the tremendous decline in the use of the confessional has led to the clergy's decreasing interest in it as a forum for spiritual direction. Meanwhile certain monasteries, retreat centers, and Catholic universities have developed programs for training spiritual directors. Religious orders have absorbed some of this recent interest in spiritual direction, with the orders of women, it may safely be said, far outstripping the clerical orders in this regard.

One thing is clear: the practice of *baqqesh*, for more than a few moments, does not come easily for most, even when combined with *greeting*. Jesus' most intimate disciples, Peter, James, and John, could not "watch and pray" one hour with Jesus (Mark 14:32–42). Through the rosary we will increasingly desire to give a better service of *baqqesh*, and this in turn will send us naturally in the direction of simple ascetic practices.

9. Prayer of Praise

Whatever our experience of God, we will doubtless agree that God is fundamental—or, using a different metaphor, the Supreme Being. Because God is indeed supreme, he is superlatively beautiful, good, and knowing. If we catch even a tiny glimpse of his beauty, goodness, and intelligence, we find ourselves praising him, which is why prayer so often takes the form of praise. And praise, when flowing from a sincere sense of wonder, is a powerful stimulus to meditation.

There are two ways to praise: direct and indirect. Even though the rosary concentrates our focus on God, it does so very gently, particularly at first, using a combination of direct and indirect approaches. For example, the rosary shows us certain aspects (the mysteries) of the life of Christ and asks us to praise Christ. Christ's mysteries are, of course, very human things, ranging from his conception to his death and afterlife. At first glance, it might not appear so obvious that to praise these human events, even in a life as noble as Christ's, is to praise God. But we take the position that, in the life of Christ, we have God's idea of how a human life ought to be lived.

To praise that life is to praise the mind of God, to praise, then, God himself. To study that life is to catch glimpses of the beauty, goodness, and intelligence of divinity. But since these gems are set in the day-by-day life of Christ, they can be called an *indirect* treasury of motives for praising God.

Equally important is the fact that the rosary does not ask us to direct all praise directly to God, though that is the ultimate goal of our communication. Rather, we may praise Christ and God *to a third person.*

Sometimes we feel that indirect praise is somehow less worthy than praise of the direct sort. But this is simply not the case, as we can verify by consulting our own experiences. Very often we try to praise a beloved friend, parent, child, or spouse to his or her face and find that our thoughts and feelings are slow in coming. But when we praise that same beloved person to some other person, especially a friend, we frequently find our powers of insight and expression becoming more intense.

The best known word of praise in Jewish and Christian tradition is the Hebrew word *halleluia.* It means "praise the Lord," and it makes sense only as spoken to others. So, while we recognize that direct praise is in some ways ideal, this in no way lessens the special effectiveness of indirect praise. The truth seems to be that a combination of approaches is best, and it is just such a combination that the rosary provides.

The person to whom the rosary directs a great deal of its praise of God and Christ is Mary, the mother of Jesus. She was, according to our tradition, well schooled in prayer and *baqqesh,* and is, therefore, a most appropriate person to whom we can praise God.

But it is especially when we praise God in the life of Christ, as described above, that Mary's credibility as our listener soars: she was a disciple of Jesus Christ—in fact, we will try to show that her life was a portrait of the ideal disciple. But she was also his mother, a fact that makes an intuitive, unanalytical appeal to many of our latent meditative powers.

Moreover, the New Testament of the Bible shows Mary as a person dedicated to meditation (Luke 2:19). This fact gives us a further motive for choosing her as one to keep in view as we meditate.

Mary, of course, passed from this world almost twenty centuries ago. Can the dead *really* hear us, or do we have here only a useful stimulus to meditation? Among Christians, some think the dead cannot hear us; others hold that the dead can only hear us if God makes some special provision, in particular cases, enabling them to hear us.

(It may be helpful to note in this regard that modern physics holds that the past, the world of the dead, does not vanish, but is still theoretically accessible to us at certain velocities, locations, and energy states.)

Number 11.C, page 21, will shed light on the availability of the dead. Ultimately, however, we must appeal to experience, and a widespread experience in Christianity affirms that Mary is, more than any other disciple of Christ, the person who seems specially commissioned for the role of Listener. If God ever planned to give us a Listener, someone for all ages, who would be a fellow disciple more keen to hear praise of God and Jesus Christ than any of us, surely Mary is that person. If our meditation is truly a pathway into the real, then there ought to be reality about Mary. But a doubting reader will have to prove this personally.

10. Intercessory Prayer

The purpose of prayer, as was mentioned above, is not to get our way with God. But prayer *does* work. God responds to prayer; such is the experience of the ages. We may but rarely recognize his response at the time, as it may take a form not immediately seen as connected to our prayer, but God does respond. Indeed, sometimes he may actually be seen to fulfill a request. More often he responds more delicately, knowing that what we pray for is something we really would not want if we could see all its implications.

But because God *does* respond to prayer, a conversation of sorts arises between the praying person and God. As described above (page 5), we pray, mainly, with words, and God answers, mainly, with actions. Through this language of events, God reveals more and more of his true nature. Gently, as was said in the discussion of hope (number 6, page 9), he teaches us to want the sorts of things that he wants so that he can answer our prayers ever more convincingly. It comes to this: God, who could easily have his way with the world, prefers to teach us to hope in advance for the very things he wishes to do for us. In this way, humanity is brought into the process by which God achieves things. Human prayers, while they do not constrain God, become almost a condition for his action and thus become part of that action.

We often pray on behalf of others. We often ask others to pray for us. Such prayer is called "intercession." It can be, certainly, a wholesome practice, effective in some important ways. But it is ridiculous to think that God would not do what was best for us unless cajoled into it by someone who prays better than we do. Intercessory prayer, if it is to mean anything, must come from hearts well schooled in the ways of God, hearts that know that prayers are healthy and effective when they tend to actions that God already wishes to do.

The word *intercession* has done mischief here. It comes from the Latin and refers to one individual being a "go-between" (*cedo*: "go"; *inter*: "between") for another. Thus has arisen the very unfortunate idea that one person can almost extort from God some favor that he had already decided against. The idea, as I have said, is ridiculous.

To understand what intercession really is we would have to be very close to God. We ask the prayers of a good intercessor not so that we can get our way with God but so that the selfish or mistaken portions of our prayer may be transformed or deleted by being filtered through another's prayer. Our first cry into the limitless unknown asserted our kinship with all reality; intercessors put that kinship into action.

It is commonly held by Christians that Jesus is so close to God that his intercessory prayer is uniquely important. In a different sense, Christians also believe that other human beings, in varying ways and degrees, can be asked to take up our causes, purifying them in the process. Catholic and Orthodox Christians, and many others as well, further believe that the prayers of Mary, mother of Jesus and Listener par excellence, are especially suitable for us, notwithstanding the fact that she, and many other God-filled intercessors, are no longer visibly present.

Why would God accept our prayers as purified by others when it is our own purification that he so much desires? Perhaps because, while intercessory prayer is partly the prayer of another, it is still initiated *by us* and thus gives God a chance to teach us a language of events. And the person who requests others to pray also gradually learns what it is in his or her own prayer that needs correction.

In non-Western cultures it is by no means rare that meditations are carried out with keen awareness of communion with the deceased. There seems to be an instinctive recognition that time does not exist in the world of God, that the spiritual powers developed by persons long dead are still available and relevant. It is part of the irony of our Western culture, however, that privileges we readily concede to peoples of the nonindustrialized world we fail to see as possibly applicable or active in our own midst.

For the Protestant Christian, there may not seem sufficient theological grounds for bringing Mary so intimately into our meditation. These grounds will be developed more fully in my treatment of the individual mysteries and in number 11.C, on page 21. Meanwhile I repeat the point with which this book opened: the best proof of the rosary is its own effectiveness.

11. Does One Have to Be a Catholic to Use the Rosary?

There are three aspects to this question: God, Christ, Mary.

A. God

The central prayer of the rosary (central in importance, though not numerically) is the prayer taught by Jesus himself, the so-called "Lord's Prayer" or "Our Father." The fundamental assumption of this prayer is that God loves us (which is one reason for calling him "Father") and that he is promoting a kingdom of love and justice among us. It greatly energizes meditation to look thus trustingly upon the mysterious presence to whom we raise our minds and hearts.

Certainly a person who shared none of the trustful view of God taught by Moses and Jesus would be unable to enter rosary meditation. But it would be rather easy to show that all the great meditative traditions imply an open acceptance of reality. Meanwhile, we Christians admit we are but beginners on the road of trust.

Rosary users from outside Christianity would not, obviously, share the full trinitarian view of God professed by Christian orthodoxy. How could such meditators profit from the rosary with its implied, but pervasive, trinitarianism? The trinitarian doctrine, to say the very least, does encourage us to hold onto more than one experience of the divine. Exactly here trinitarianism makes room for the manifold aspects of the divine acknowledged by other religions.

Trinitarianism is thus one of the integrative, nonanalytical features of Christian meditation. Raimundo Panikkar, the Hindu Catholic priest (to cite only one example), has written extensively on the compatibility of trinitarianism with Hinduism and Buddhism.[13]

Rather than say that one must be a professing trinitarian to use the rosary, it may be sufficient to say that the rosary itself is a way of discovering the trinitarian (as well as the unitive) aspects of the divine. Thus a rosary user from outside Christianity should be careful not to deny the trinitarian view at the outset, shutting the doors to various experiences of the divine. The trinitarian teaching itself seems to have been formulated, originally, to prevent such sweeping denials. And, although Judaism and Islam are totally monotheistic (as Christianity also professes to be), these two religions are certainly sensitive to various aspects of divine reality. Orthodox Christians, of course, do accept the Trinity explicitly, and this is an essential part not only of their religion but also of their rosary meditation.

B. Jesus Christ

The fifteen mysteries of the rosary are scenes from the life of Jesus; they certainly portray him as the greatest person whom God has made accessible to humanity at large. What can a non-Christian make of that?

Some Christians affirm that "Jesus is Lord" in utter perfection, his greatness outstripping the founders of other religions in every conceivable way. For them, even Jesus' personal magnetism and rhetorical ability must surpass all others known to humanity. In this book I begin more simply: Jesus is the one person whose life and teaching best appreciates and "saves" the central truths and deeds of other teachers. Even this more limited claim would imply, of course, Jesus' towering uniqueness. But it does not demand that Jesus was necessarily the most poetic of all prophets, the most persuasive of all orators, the most analytical of all philosophers, the most successful of teachers, the canniest of

---

[13] See especially *The Trinity and the Religious Experience of Man* (New York: Orbis Books, 1973).

leaders. Far from belittling other founders, the rosary user can glory in their triumphs.

Most Christians, of course, (and Catholics among them) go further than merely saying that Jesus is the one person who best saves the truths and deeds of all others. Rather, Christian teaching holds that Jesus is an act of God in a more direct sense, that he is a human being whose existence, at root, rests not on a created basis such as the rest of us enjoy but directly on the divine existence of the eternal Word of God.

One suspects that adherents of other great world religions often can understand this point better than do we who were educated in the modern West. The first Christians (themselves decidedly premodern, pre-Western) came to believe that Jesus had received the Divine Name (Philippians 2:9) because they experienced Jesus as one through whom they enjoyed convincing access to the Divine. But, over the first four centuries A.D., there was increasingly felt the need to express this experience in a ringing affirmation about Jesus similar to that by which early Israel had professed its experience of its national God to be an experience of the supreme Lord: "Hear, O Israel, the Lord is our God, the Lord is one!"

The only way a statement of this sort could be achieved against the prevailing philosophical background of late Greco-Roman antiquity was to affirm Divine Existence as the basis of the man Jesus. Religions around the world know what it is to reach the divine through the individual; they can perhaps at least sympathize with the Christian need to express this in existential terms. It is more apt to be the Westerner, with no practical experience of meditation, and a brutal willingness to separate meditation from science, who cannot put divine and human together in a single frame.

Most Christians have not regretted these existentialist affirmations of the fourth and fifth centuries, which prevented the Christian experience from retreating into safe obscurity. But already in the fourth century, and ever since, these affirmations have indeed often been rejected in the West precisely by those who were *mere* theorists, willing to separate theology from life, liturgy, and meditation.

We Catholics, meanwhile, ought to be honest with ourselves and admit that many of those who use the rosary most effectively have little idea about the statements in theology books or even (alas!) in catechisms. If we waited until we could describe Jesus acceptably in terms of doctrine before taking up the rosary, we would be denying ourselves one of the most effective instruments for understanding him: the rosary itself. At the outset, as I have said, it is important that anyone using the rosary not deny the traditional doctrines (which are understood by few in any case). The meditator will thus avoid barring himself or herself from new paths leading to the Center.

An analogy from physics may help. The greatest discoveries of physics (relativity and quantum mechanics, for example) are but imperfectly understood, even by great physicists. But however imperfectly understood, these discoveries are effectively used in the uncovering of further truths and in the design of new techniques and inventions. Using these discoveries helps to appreciate them. It would be sophomoric to deny the new discoveries simply because their deepest meaning continually eludes us.

C. Mary

The rosary sees Mary as the principal Listener among the disciples of Christ. This prominence for Mary will seem strange to many Protestant Christians. Catholicism, further, teaches that Mary had a special suitability to be the mother of Jesus Christ, that parenting is important, even for a Messiah. Only the perusal of the fifteen mysteries of the rosary, which occupies a great portion of this book (chapters 4 and 5), can determine the extent to which a non-Catholic Christian will agree. With their great devotion to the Bible, Protestants may be pleased to learn, however, that thirteen of the rosary's fifteen mysteries are taken directly from the New Testament.

There is, of course, a subtle difficulty here. Protestant Christians are relatively unaccustomed to talking to any of the dead (except Jesus himself)—not even, in many cases, their own departed family members. In view of the many abuses to which this custom had given rise in the late Middle Ages, the Protestant Reformers successfully, and quite understandably, rooted it out of their communities.

Much of the difficulty comes from our trying to picture the situation in linear terms: we imagine ourselves as moving along one time line (our life history), while God moves along his own, different, time line. Then we think of prayer as leaping, like a radio signal, from the human line to the divine line. While many people are able, through long practice, to think of prayer in this way, the picture thus presented scarcely gives us confidence that mere humans, like Mary or any of the departed, could also hear our tiny signals.

God, however, is not on a time line. There is no past, present, or future with him. But because God's world has not yet been revealed to us, he is in *our* future. He comes to us on *our* time line, moving down it from what seems his future to our present location, always bringing his world as it "will" be. He is not on a neighboring parallel line to which prayer must leap; rather he is on our line, touching our "now," offering us early contact with himself as he "will" be. Prayer is opening ourselves to receive God's future-made-present.

God's world-to-come, however, includes all the "saints." These are beings who once lived on a time line but who no longer work out their meanings on a daily basis. They have their meanings now assumed into the timeless validity of God's life. In other words, if ever, in some future beatitude, all intelligent beings will communicate, they already *are* communicating in the world with which God approaches us in prayer.

Protestant Christians, of course, have been in the forefront of those who have understood that the fulfillment of God's Kingdom is already operative. But Catholics, too, hold that his final Kingdom is already available, especially in prayer and sacrament. It is but a short step further to see that the saints come back from the future with God and are close to us, though only in God.

Karl Rahner[14] gave us a powerful explanation of this matter: we are all called to love each other as part of the essence of loving God. The "communion of saints," which *is* this mutual love, is not shattered by death. In a real sense, we love the departed saints (and the departed sinners!), and they love us. (This is true whether or not they know us individually.) And their love for us, like all love in life or death, is integrated with their love of God and involves a constant reference to God. The saints, in other words, are already interceding for us whether we ask it of them or not. Further (and here I am adding to Rahner's thoughts), the love that the saints have for us is something God wants us to experience, to become increasingly aware of. And it is no sign of spiritual maturity to fail to note *any* source of supporting love, whether terrestrial or celestial in origin.

Why Mary? The fifteen mysteries will (or will not!) teach us that. And even if there were no reason to believe that God had selected Mary as Listener, the matter can be put in another way: Mary is the person most widely chosen by *us* to be our Listener. When God allows her to be the Listener, he honors the human family that selects her. It has often been well said that Mary's special role results not from her own merits but from her function as mother of Christ. We are here extending that principle: her role also results from her function as the mother selected by the "Body of Christ," as his disciples are collectively known.

I have developed this section somewhat more fully than others in this primarily practical book. The reason is simple: the whole method of the rosary is to lift our powers toward persons. But if we conceive of these persons as unreal, or out of reach, we will fail to be deeply energized by the rosary. Thus, neither Catholic nor non-Catholic can hope to use the rosary if God, Christ, or Mary is taken as merely figuratively available. At the same time, however, we can recommend that the rosary be actually tried so that the user may eventually discover how real or unreal these persons may be.

---

[14] Metz and Rahner, *The Courage to Pray*, op. cit., 31–87, particularly 70, 71.

12. Repetition in Religion and Meditation

The heart of the rosary is the "Our Father," the prayer formulated by Jesus himself. But the prayer known as the "Hail Mary" outnumbers the Our Father ten to one in the rosary. For some, this may seem an unacceptable ratio, giving too much prominence to Mary.

The Our Father is the high point of the rosary. The Hail Marys, however numerous, are meant to enhance the quality of our use of the Our Father. When the *Queen Elizabeth II* docks at New York it may be accompanied by as many as ten tugboats, yet no one is confused as to which ship is the *Queen*. Almost from the start, one can expect the quality of one's use of the Our Father to improve, and the Hail Marys will be seen as justifying their number.

Beginners are sometimes dismayed to learn that the framework of the rosary consists of 150 Hail Marys divided into fifteen mysteries, each containing ten Hail Marys. Each mystery (or "decade," as it is called) is preceded by an Our Father and concluded by a short doxology (see the chart on page xviii). This is a goodly lot of repetition, even if one follows the dominant custom of meditating through only one third of the rosary each day. (A third part of the rosary, consisting of five decades [mysteries], is technically called a "chaplet.") It seems pointless to try to tell the inexperienced that this repetition soon ceases to be monotonous and, indeed, becomes effective and desirable. But some explanation of *why* such repetition is so satisfactory will fit nicely here.

Repetition is the closest thing we humans have to time travel. I cannot go back to my childhood and reenter the wonderful birthday party that I was then given, but I may see to it that my child has a good party. In so doing, I may bring some of the spirit and a few of the details from my past into the present. Similarly, people re-create Christmases, Thanksgivings, and wedding receptions. When these experiments in time travel fail to please, it is often because repetition succeeded too well and re-created a moment not suitable for the present. But such attempts *do* please often enough to make repetition popular.

In religion, it is thought vital that each generation be brought into the events, now long past, that began the history of a particular people or religious family. The Jewish Passover and the Catholic Mass, especially the Mass of Easter, do that: both are reenactments, repetitions.

But it is true that there is more here than the simple effectiveness of reminiscing. At the frontiers of the human mind, time really does cease. A past event retains its power of communication, reaching out to us through the symbols of its own repetition. But communications, modern physics shows, are not merely symbolism. They really affect the nature of physical relationships around them. Much more do they affect the human spirit (minds and hearts) and human relations.

An artist once told me that the trouble with many inexperienced painters is that they only work a canvas over once or twice. A good oil painting, he assured me, might be painted six or eight times, layer upon layer, before the artist might arrive at the point to which his or her art had been leading from the beginning. The same may be said of human actions in general. Because we cannot achieve maximum intensity of knowing and willing (mind and heart) by a single effort, we go over the same ground repeatedly. Such activity may be very boring to the bystander who is compelled to watch. But it is not boring to the actor. As the mind becomes adept at meditation, each opportunity to repeat can be welcomed and enjoyed, much as an expert with a basketball enjoys throwing ball after ball through the hoop in seemingly endless practice.

13. The Rosary, a Gateway to Contemplation

I have defined meditation (page 6) as "a way of tapping the tremendous resources of our minds and wills for the purpose of giving us a new and deeper contact with reality." Taken by themselves, these words seem to imply that meditation is mainly *our* activity: *we* follow a certain way or method of tapping our powers; *we* then exercise those powers in a new contact with reality. But a corrective is in order: reality itself (which includes God!) has a way of taking over; indeed, reality (including God) can ultimately be seen as having been active from the first. The traditional word designating our openness to the activity that is *not* primarily ours, but comes from Reality itself, is *contemplation*.

The great bulk of this book is filled with details about the rosary as *our* active method of meditation. There is thus a real danger that we will lose sight of contemplation (see chapter 6). Because contemplation is necessarily discussed only after the details of the rosary's method, we may in the meantime be tempted to forget that God (Reality), not self, is the major force in the rosary. As we proceed, there will be reminders of the necessity of a contemplative outlook throughout. Long before we arrive at chapter 6, the rosary user will have understood that his or her goal is to absorb the details of rosary meditation so that the mind and will can, in an uncluttered way, be increasingly open to the action of the Real. Contemplation is an essential part of meditation, and not something at which one arrives only at the end of the road. All human beings have some experience of it, whether or not they follow a way of meditation.

2

The Prayers of the Rosary

The ingredients of the rosary are of great antiquity. The practice of *baqqesh* (see number 7) is doubtless prehistoric; at all events it is attested in the Old Testament and even earlier. The Our Father was the prayer of Jesus some two thousand years ago, but even he drew on materials familiar from the already ancient Books of Exodus and Numbers. The words of the Hail Mary are mainly from the Gospel of Luke, and thus are rooted in Christian origins. Of the fifteen mysteries of the rosary (the events in Christ's life that form the backdrop for rosary meditation), thirteen are from the New Testament, while the two remaining were eventually seen in the others.

14. The Basic Materials and a Little History

We meet the mysteries only in chapter 4, but a little of their history is needed here. Of the thirteen mysteries already in the New Testament, all can be found in the writings of St. Luke (author of the Gospel according to Luke and of the Acts of the Apostles). Not only does Luke give us the mysteries later borrowed by the rosary, but he presents them in such a way as to encourage meditation on them. They are full of seekings and searchings; they portray Mary as a meditative person and, in fact, contain the words of the Hail Mary. So effective are these scenes as sketched by Luke that early tradition claimed he was an artist. Certainly he was a literary artist and a proponent of meditation. The Lucan mysteries have always been subjects of meditation and of Christian art. Thus we may say, speaking broadly, that two major elements of rosary meditation, the mysteries and *baqqesh*, have had a continuous history of cooperation beginning with Luke himself.

After Luke, the tradition of *baqqesh* reappears most clearly in the lay monasticism of the early centuries. The monks and nuns of the Syrian and Egyptian deserts trained themselves in "awaiting the resurrection," an art that reappeared in European monasticism. In Celtic monasticism, for example, individual monks or nuns sometimes occupied tiny isles in the sea to practice the Waiting. Throughout Christendom, in fact, worship faced east, the traditional direction for seeking the returning Lord.[15] During these centuries, most of Luke's mysteries became the subjects of special Church festivals. They, with other gospel scenes, were celebrated in sermons, mystery plays, paintings, and, eventually, stained glass windows. In the daily recitation of the Psalms it became the custom to recall Luke's mysteries, or some of them, at the end of each psalm.[16]

The History of Repetitive Prayer

The use of repetitive prayer as a basis of meditation is a rosary technique to be sharply distinguished from the method of meditating by means of Luke's mysteries. The use of repetitive prayer

---

[15] An influential summary of the history of early mystical meditation and its relationship to the ascetical life in and out of monasticism was Margaret Smith's *The Way of the Mystics: The Early Christian Mystics and the Rise of the Sufis* (Oxford: Oxford University Press, 1978). As the title indicates, Smith's book traced mystic meditation's influence on the mystics of Islam.

[16] See "The Rosary" in Michael O'Carroll, *Theotokos: A Theological Encyclopedia of the Blessed Virgin Mary* (Wilmington, Del.: Michael Glazier, 1982), 313, 314.

is far older than the New Testament; humanity's oldest written records, those of Egypt and Mesopotamia, already attest to it. Especially popular were repetitive greetings not unlike our use of "Our Father" and "Hail Mary . . . blessed art thou." Acclamations and choral responses were equally well known in the Israelite temple at Jerusalem. Christians also, from an early time, have devised litanies in which God or the saints are invoked in repetitive lists of names or in which a single name is repeated with varying choral responses. Although Mary's role as Listener is attested in many ancient hymns, the use of the Hail Mary for repetitive greetings seems to have become widespread only in the eleventh century, at a time when the Our Father was similarly used. The greetings were apparently taken with great seriousness, often being accompanied by genuflections or even prostrations. Simultaneously came the custom of completing fixed numbers of greetings (usually 150, in imitation of the number of psalms); one prayed with the aid of a knotted cord or a string of beads.

The rosary as we know it was created by the merging of these two streams: the method of meditation against a background of repeated words of praise, and the popular Lucan scenes of meditation, which are so effective for *baqqesh*. Gradually, the mysteries, already used for the Psalms, came to be recalled at the end of each Hail Mary. By the end of the fourteenth century came our present method of recalling the mysteries only once for each ten Hail Marys, marked off by an Our Father. In the meantime, the Hail Mary had received a concluding section ("Holy Mary," etc.) comparable to those used in litanies.

It is not particularly accurate to think that the rosary was only discovered five or six hundred years ago. From the beginning, the pursuit of the life of the spirit had been exceedingly popular, but enthusiasts were generally thrown upon their own devices for obtaining a mix of meditative elements such as *baqqesh*, mysteries, and the like. The uniqueness of the rosary, perhaps, consists in the rapid popularization of a single method. Without even aiming at meditation in a technical sense, hundreds of thousands of people were quickly introduced to a method that might have taken them a lifetime to discover by themselves.

Many people have begun the use of the rosary only to give it up soon after, discouraged because they could not combine the repeated prayers with the fifteen mysteries. But, like anything else, the rosary must be mastered in stages. First, one must be able to say the Our Fathers and Hail Marys very well; then, and only then, should one add the fifteen mysteries, which will be, in the end, so important.

Perhaps to allay fears that 150 Hail Marys will be boring, we have often been told that it is the mysteries, rather than the prayers that are important. The result has been that we have tried to meditate on the mysteries while not paying much attention to the words of the prayers, which soon became prattle. We have been unaware that, in meditation, it is not at all impossible to think of two things at once, provided both are really attended to. But this, for us who have lost the ability to meditate, requires building up slowly, one thing at a time: the prayers first, then the mysteries. If we ignore the prayers we are ignoring the *greetings*, the basic methodological element in the rosary.

It cannot be stressed enough that we are not a meditative society. Meditations that may seem child's play to an Egyptian peasant are very difficult for the harassed and hurried citizens of technopolis. We must recapture skills we have not exercised since childhood, and we will have to be patient with ourselves. I recommend beginning with only a few Our Fathers and Hail Marys at a time, proceeding slowly and with great deliberateness. A generous portion of time must be set aside each day (several short sessions are preferable to one very long session).

15. Waiting: Preparing for Prayer

In number 16, below, we begin our consideration of the Our Father. But in prayer there is no such thing as a mere rehearsal: even to read about a prayer is already to use it, and to use it without preparation is folly. Thus, before beginning number 16, the reader must actually prepare by doing some *baqqesh*, and especially that part of *baqqesh* that is called "Waiting" (*qawweh*). Waiting has been briefly described at the end of number 7, on *baqqesh*, where it was compared with the practice of placing oneself in the presence of God.

We cannot see, sense, or imagine God; with this in mind, place yourself in his presence and know that he is there. *Wait* for him to act.

What might God do? He *might* end the world while you are waiting. He *might* send into your room a friend or a foe, some great joy or some great suffering. You may, in the next few moments, be given a new obligation, a new privilege, a new commission, a new vocation.

It is probable that God will do none of these things in the next few moments. But he *might*. Certainly he will do something: if not something in your presence, then something elsewhere about which you may learn later on. He has a creator's love for you and is totally aware of you. You are his servant, his messenger, his friend, his child. In a way, you even love him. You are ready, waiting upon his will.

But for how long? How long can you wait? How long can you remain in his unseen presence aware of nothing except that he may suddenly enter your life? Try to wait attentively for perhaps half a minute before you begin to read number 16.

16. The Our Father

WORD (of greeting)	**Our Father who art in heaven,**
BLESSING	**Hallowed be thy Name.** **Thy Kingdom come,** **thy will be done,** **on earth as it is in heaven.**

CRY

Give us this day our daily bread,
and forgive us our trespasses
as we forgive those who
trespass against us.
Lead us not into temptation,
but deliver us from evil. Amen.

WORD (of Greeting): **Our Father who art in heaven**

In all systems of meditation, from whatever tradition, there is always something *given* to the seeker. In one system it may be the simple human ability, given to all the living, to breathe in and out. In another system it may be the power to hum a musical note. Still other systems are based on our given ability to notice something or on our ability not to notice it. In the rosary, we make use of the power, given to all of us, to greet someone, to begin the process of communication.

The seeker can transcend the limitations of self (*raise* oneself) only by acknowledging that there is something that is not self-made but is attainable only through Gift. The various traditions speak of "the Force," "the Spirit," "Grace," or something similar. Yet these gifts are always something simple, like breathing or humming or greeting. They are gifts because we do not teach them to ourselves: they are among the givens of human existence, coming to us from those among whom we live. But these simple gifts are also divine, for they are as basic as existence itself, that elemental gift of God.

If you can breathe, you can begin to meditate. If you can hum or greet, you can begin to meditate. A great burden is lifted from us when we realize that the first steps in meditation do not require us to muster great or unusual force, but are givens.

In Judeo-Christian-Islamic tradition, and hence in the rosary, one begins with a greeting. In the Our Father, for example, we greet divinity, and we are given a word to use: *Father*. The Bible does not present the word *Father* as the divine name itself, but as a kind of substitute for it. There are many such substitutes in Biblical tradition, but *Father* is the one preferred by Jesus of Nazareth. *Father* is a term of love and trust: our tradition has held, at least from the time of Moses, that God can be trusted. Since meditation is an act of communication, trusting (letting go) is particularly important.

But let us return to the idea of a simple gift. To appreciate the situation better, let's construct a myth. Let's pretend that some words, some greetings, are so profound as to originate only in divinity. Such words, let's say, are spoken by God from eternity. They enter our world and begin searching for persons willing to pronounce them.

We could say, picturing the situation rather crudely, that God searches for lips willing to open, to liberate these words. God alone can pronounce greetings appropriate for God, but if we willingly allow these words to escape from us, we appropriate to ourselves the action of communication so that we are not merely puppets. Yet because the Word of greeting is clearly a gift, one of the simple things upon which meditation can be built, we can properly regard it as coming from God and seeking expression through us. Thus Saint Paul wrote (Romans 8:15; Galatians 4:6) that the Spirit of God is within us teaching us to cry *Abba* (Aramaic: "Father").

Since Jesus spoke Aramaic, he undoubtedly had *Abba* in mind when he gave us the Our Father. C. H. Dodd and others have established that *Abba* is a familiar form of the word *Father,* implying approachability, trust, intimacy. The addition of pronouns (*our* Father, *my* Father, etc.) further serves to convert the bare noun *Father* into an instrument of address, of greeting.

I have spoken of humanity's cry into the limitless unknown. From this point the reader should experiment with voicing this cry as "Father." It will be good to signal to the Father in various situations, writing down your thoughts and feelings. Is your Waiting easier now that you call God "Father"?

One Word,One Blessing, One Cry

Let's suppose that we have decided to seek (*baqqesh*) the divinity and that we have been allowed only three attempts. (There is a certain economy in things divine, which may be why so many myths and wonder tales grant but three wishes, three guesses, and so forth.) We have already been granted one word of greeting (the previous section), and now find that we have remaining (this section and the next) one blessing and one cry.

We have seen that the "one word" is *Father*. The "one blessing" emerges in three almost synonymous phrases:[17]

ONE BLESSING	**Hallowed be thy Name.** **Thy Kingdom come,** **thy will be done,** **on earth as it is in heaven.**

We began the Our Father with a few moments of the Waiting, out of which came Greeting, but eventually we learn to keep the Waiting intact through the whole Our Father. At this point, Waiting opens into one of its companions: Seeking (*baqqesh*). Out of Waiting we begin to look for God's action, some revelation/event of God's Name/Kingdom/Will.

This section is called a blessing. In our Western tradition, blessing has unfortunately become very passive, something we receive from God or clergy or, rarely, from others.We seldom do any blessing ourselves. In the Bible, however, blessing is simply the use of good words, while cursing is the use of words depicting

---

[17] If the phrases of the Our Father were not almost synonymous but, rather, differed from phrase to phrase, they would involve us in discursive reasoning. Many fine prayers contain discursive reasoning, but all such lack the simplicity needed for rosary meditation. See Anthony Bloom, *Beginning to Pray*, pages 60, 61, for a description of how the famous "Jesus Prayer" used by the Orthodox Churches functions as a single motion, rich in meaning but nondiscursive. See also Catoir, *Enjoy the Lord*, op.cit., pages 86–94.

In his *Spiritual Exercises*, St. Ignatius of Loyola recommends ("The Third Method of Prayer") a rhythm in which each breath will correspond to a single word of the prayer. In the rosary a number of words will flow from each breath, yet they will all be one intention, one motion.

disaster. Biblical tradition not only encourages us to bless, but calls upon us to bless God himself, as we do here. The ancient notion was that, after having been blessed by us, God would reciprocate with good words of his own, which, of course, would actually be good events.

Blessings can be stated as hopes ("Hallowed be thy Name") or as facts ("Holy is your Name"). Very often the verb ("be" or "is") is left out, with the result that both meanings are included. In blessing God there is no difference between "be" and "is," for a pure hope is already a fact in his world. A *baqqesh* (searching with hope) is already an act of praise.

Hallowed be thy Name

Modern sciences have been successful in analyzing things into their several parts. But now one frequently hears scientists say that we need a holistic approach, enabling us to confront any given being in its totality.

A symbol represents the whole of a being. A snapshot, for example, may represent the whole nature of my friend very effectively, even though only a portion of the body is represented. For preindustrial ("primitive") people, the most effective symbol of any being is its name. Its name conjures up its whole reality.

When we confront God's Name, then, we are not trying to analyze God into his several powers or qualities or even to compare him with something else. We are striving to contact the whole of him.

Again, for preindustrial humanity, a name, like any symbol, gives access to a being. We recall that in the Book of Exodus God is said to have done his people the kindness of revealing his Name to them (Exodus 3). He asks only that his Name not be used "in vain" (to no good purpose: Exodus 20). By putting the language of our ancestors into modern phrases, God, in fact, is giving access to himself and asks only that we not abuse the relationship that he offers us.

The word *hallowed* means "revered." In the language of the Bible and of Jesus Christ, we hallow something when, in recognition of the fascinating and awe-inspiring effect it is having on us, we give it a special place. Thus the Sabbath day was to be hallowed (made special) because it is the day above all others when we seek God, who both fascinates us and fills us with awe. Similarly, the mo-ment when we call upon the Name that opens up our relationship with God must be a moment that we treasure and treat as special ("holy").

Thy Kingdom come, thy will be done,
on earth as it is in heaven.

Here are two further phrases by which we stretch toward God. Their basic meaning, though, is not different from "hallowed be thy Name," for, according to the teachings of Jesus, when God gives his Name he also gives, as far as we will allow him to do so, his Kingdom and his Will. In the Old Testament, the word *will* signifies God's good will. The probable stress here, then, is not on the grim difficulties we may face if we attempt to do God's will. Similarly, the "Kingdom," refers primarily to God's attempts to foster a realm of justice and peace *among us*. It is not so much a prayer to have heaven *replace* earth, as a prayer to allow earth to be like heaven.

Here is the irony of the blessing: we wish success to God's Name, Kingdom, and Will, but then we realize that all three are benefits God is extending to us. The Our Father is giving us a new perspective on reality: it is of our nature to receive. Even now, we, the people of the earth, are being shaped in accord with a marvelous plan. We begin to sense that even our being is a supported being. Our task is to learn to accept.

ONE CRY

Give us this day our daily bread,
and forgive us our trespasses
as we forgive those who trespass against us.
Lead us not into temptation,
but deliver us from evil. Amen.

Give us this day our daily bread

The first two-thirds of the Our Father is concerned directly with God and can be truly called an act of pure worship. The last third, which begins here, is a series of petitions (constituting "one cry") on behalf of human needs. But even these petitions, because they show trust in God, give him praise. And even they are searchings for elements of his Kingdom.

Jesus may have been thinking of the daily bread from heaven ("manna," see Exodus 16:4, 5) with which God fed Israel. By asking only for sufficiency, rather than a large security for the future, we again express trust in God. We further show that we seek the advancement of his Kingdom rather than our own wealth.

Forgive us our trespasses as we forgive those who trespass against us.

Since the Kingdom of God is a community in which God's standards of love and justice are upheld, it is evident that his Kingdom would come among us if we forgave each other all offenses, real or imagined. The good will God extends to us must be extended by us to others. "Love your enemies," said Jesus, it being the only strategy by which there is any hope of abolishing hate and injury upon the earth.

Lead us not into temptation, but deliver us from evil.

God is able to catch hold of all the good threads in history and weave them together into a tapestry that is the fulfillment of the Kingdom of God. But there is also a tapestry of evil, though on a lesser scale. The evil that we humans do also tends to enter into combinations, working up to a climactic challenge to God. Jesus taught that our personal wrongdoing has wide-ranging effects, far outstripping the evil we originally had in mind when we perpetrated our misdeeds. The Bible uses words such as *contest, struggle, testing,* or *trial* to signify the climactic combination of evils—the idea being that we foolish humans will subject God to a trial. Jesus was probably thinking here of Israel's challenge to

God at Massah (Exodus 17:7), a place whose very name the Bible understands as meaning "trial." The prayer asks, then, that we not be led unprepared and unexpectedly into the gathering storm, a place like Massah where we humans will challenge God and suffer loss. ("Temptation" is surely a pale translation for "the Trial.")

If the prayer also asks that *we* not be tempted ("tried"), it is only because our lesser brushes with evil may involve us in the greater conspiracy. But we know, in fact, that we must be tested, and that God will always assist us.

Similarly, many scholars think that "deliver us from evil," should be translated "deliver us from the evil one." Here would be a reference to the belief that, in the climactic struggle in which evils combine, a being of satanic malice will assume a position of leadership. Many Christians have culled the Bible for hints as to the nature of the Evil One, but such efforts have no place in the rosary. Suffice it to say that "deliver us from evil [one]" points to the climactic struggle just as do the words "lead us not into temptation." In our meditation, these two prayers serve, in a negative way, to propel us in the same direction as do the other phrases of the Our Father: toward the Kingdom of the Father.

How do these three petitions constitute "one cry"? To understand this we need only to invoke the Hebrew concept of *shalom* ("peace"). As has often been noted, the root meaning of *shalom* is "fullness." We have peace in the Hebrew sense only when we have the fullness of blessings. The cessation of hostilities is not enough ("Lead us not into the great trial"); we must also have sufficiency (daily bread) and love (forgiveness, social justice). Our one cry is a cry for the fullness of *shalom*.

A final note: when we seek the arrival of God's Name, Kingdom, and Will (one blessing), we are expected to trust that our *baqqesh* will be effective, at least so far as we let it be. God's Kingdom *does* come to our call. The third part (one cry) reminds us that there is an appropriate way to live in the newly arrived Kingdom: with sufficiency rather than excess, with forgiveness, not hatred, for all.

17. The Hail Mary

Begin studying the Hail Mary by practicing the Waiting as in number 15, only now you must remind yourself that the invisible God is surrounded by an invisible company of his children. Know that Mary is one of the beings you cannot see, sense, or even accurately imagine.

WORD (Greeting, Lk. 1:28)	**Hail Mary, full of grace, The Lord is with thee.**
BLESSING (Praise of Christ, Lk. 1:42)	**Blessed art thou among women and blessed is the fruit of thy womb, Jesus.**
CRY (Seeking God, *baqqesh*)	**Holy Mary, Mother of God, pray for us sinners now and at the hour of our death. Amen.**

The Hail Mary is quite properly called a prayer because, in its second section (blessing), it praises Christ who is himself presented as illustrating God's love for us. Of course this praise of Christ is directed to Mary as Listener and is recited in the presence of the Father.

In the Hail Mary we move through the same stages encountered in the Our Father: there is a word of greeting followed by a blessing and a cry. We do not want to exaggerate the importance of our word/blessing/cry schema. Surely no one in ancient Israel analyzed compositions into their several parts, much less did anyone consciously follow such schemata. But the schema does fit many prayers. Even a modern communication will often ask a favor (cry) only after a greeting and well-wishing! My main purpose here is to help us to be aware of the different elements of prayer.

WORD (of Greeting): **Hail Mary, full of grace,**
the Lord is with thee.

Concerning the Our Father, I laid down a fundamental premise (page 33) as follows: the Spirit of God, Giver of Gifts, speaks an eternal word suitable for addressing God: *Abba*, "Father." In the Hail Mary, the Spirit of God speaks an eternal word suitable for addressing *humanity*.

These words are here addressed to Mary, but they are appropriate partly because, in so many ways, she is seen as the model and embodiment of redeemed humanity. Similar words had been addressed to Israel ("Daughter Zion") in the Old Testament (see, for example, Zephaniah 3:14–17 or Zechariah 9:9) and for the same reason: Israel was seen as the embodiment of redeemed humanity.

The habit of portraying a nation or a people as a woman is common throughout the world. That God should speak so graciously to Mary–the people fits perfectly with the Judeo-Christian-Islamic attitude taught since the times of Moses: God loves his people, endows her with divine favor, and bids her rejoice.

We meditators, then, begin the Hail Mary as we begin the Our Father: we prepare ourselves to initiate one of the basic activities of humanity, that of greeting. The Spirit of God has already launched the words, and they are "good words" (Latin: *evangelium;* Anglo-Saxon: *Goodspiel*), and so we willingly prepare to *evangelize* the Lady.

In the story of the Annunciation, which records these words (Luke 1:28), they are said to be words of the angel Gabriel. But, in a prior sense, they are words of the Spirit of God. For what does an angel convey, in biblical tradition, except the inspired divine words? No angel speaks from personal authority—least of all Gabriel, whose very name means "Power of God"! Thus, when we begin this prayer, we adopt the role of Gabriel, one who conveys the Spirit's best news to humanity. The major function of this word of greeting is simply to seek Mary's attention and to alert ourselves that we are seeking that attention. The theological meanings of the individual words (discussed below) are important but are secondary to their simple function.

Hail

"Hail" was a simple greeting, but in the original Greek of Luke, it had its own special meaning: something like "rejoice in favor." It was certainly not just a meaningless signal such as our words *hello* and *hi* have become.

Full of grace

"Full of grace," on the other hand, is far from the style of the usual greetings, though Greek usage did allow exalted titles for exalted individuals. Our English "full of grace" is an attempt to translate *kecharitomenē* from the Greek New Testament. While "grace" is the traditional rendering, the original means something closer to "favor," just as the word *grace* itself once meant "favor." *Kecharitomenē* further signifies, by its grammatical form, that Mary is a person who had received favor in the past, favor that was carrying over into the present. We might translate "long favored," although this makes a poor-sounding English phrase. "Many favored," another possible translation, means that the present good news is the culmination of previous favor. The expression, in any case, did not originally mean that Mary is full of supernatural grace as theologians define it (true as that is) but that Mary–the people had been singled out by divine favor, which had been operative in her life previously and was reaching a climax in the birth of Jesus.

In the Bible, Mary is implicitly compared with Hannah (Ann), the mother of Samuel, and Hannah's very name means "favor" (compare Luke 1:46, with 1 Samuel 2:1). For both women, "favor" refers to the unique motherhood they have been granted and the splendid child that has resulted.

The whole salutation, then, means something like "Rejoice in favor, Mary, you many favored one!" We must make an effort to pray the familiar words with the richer meanings of the original Greek.

The Lord is/be with thee

This phrase might seem better understood as the opening of the blessing rather than, as we indicate, a second word of greeting. Yet in fact it was a common greeting in Israel. We need not read a great deal of meaning into it, even though it suited Mary in the highest degree.

ONE BLESSING (Praise of Christ)	**Blessed art thou among women and blessed is the fruit of thy womb, Jesus.**

We have here another blessing, like the corresponding part of the Our Father, as even the opening word indicates. The verbs "art" and "is" are not in the original, thus providing the ambiguity of fact versus hope that is characteristic of all blessings. Because a blessing is made of "good words," it is also a prayer of praise (see number 9, page 14). Praise, more than any other act of a human being, lifts us up and out of self and so is ideal for meditation. The praise here, of course, is of Jesus Christ and is spoken to his mother.

Both halves of this "praise of Christ" are meant to praise Jesus. Even the first half, which seems to focus on Mary, is not meant chiefly as a compliment to her. "Blessed art thou among women" echoes a traditional Jewish blessing for a mother after childbirth. It means something like "You are to be congratulated! What a fine child this is, which will cause other women to bless you!" Although it congratulates the mother, the focus is on her child. In the languages of ancient Israel, moreover, it was customary for one poetic phrase to echo the idea of the previous phrase. Finally, in the same ancient languages, there was a scarcity of words meaning "because." So the little word *and* was often understood to mean "because." We would be perfectly justified, therefore, in translating this phrase: "Blessed art thou among women *because* blessed is the fruit of thy womb, Jesus." We may do this occasionally to give ourselves the correct understanding.

As a practical matter, it is wise to make a mental pause before beginning this section (at least if we are novices at rosary meditation). Having greeted Mary and, as it were, aroused her attention for the purpose of hearing her son praised, we must be careful actually to think of her son before we proceed. Everyone knows at least one praiseworthy aspect of the life and character of Jesus of Nazareth, and it is important to refer to something of the kind here; otherwise our praise will not be real. The intent even of "Blessed art thou" is, as we have said, to praise the child.

Some may suppose that Mary will be neglected if at least the first half of this praise is not directed mainly to her. But to argue in that fashion is to ignore our whole tradition about Mary. She is not interested in her own glory, but she is supremely interested in having Jesus receive praise. Of course Mary has a special place in the scheme of things: no one else was called upon to conceive, bear, nurture, educate, and form Jesus the Messiah. But had Mary been given to boasting, her boast would have been in Jesus Christ; we do not honor her if we do not acknowledge that fact.

Jesus

The mention of the name *Jesus* at the end of the second section is a wonderful help to our meditative process: Jesus, now, is with God, his Father, so we are led to refocus our attention on the Father and on Jesus with the Father. This is useful, for the next (third) section of the Hail Mary is directed to the Father and looks for Jesus in the Father.

ONE CRY

Holy Mary, Mother of God,
pray for us sinners now
and at the hour of our death.
Amen.

Clearly, this section called the "Cry," which begins with a renewed greeting (Holy Mary), is a section of intercessory prayer (recall number 10, page 16). It can be described as a purification of our prayers by their being merged into Mary's. We know that we are beginners in meditation and prayer. We know, too, that we understand Christ and God very imperfectly. So we merge our prayers "out into" the stream of Mary's prayers, that she may amplify the worthy elements of our prayer and filter out the unworthy.

This third section of the Hail Mary is sometimes belittled: unlike the first two sections, it is not a quotation from the Bible. It is neither the word of God nor the praise of Christ.

With attention and care, however, this section has unique power for the quick enlargement of the meditative life within us, for it requires us to attend to, or seek (*baqqesh*), two persons at once, and one of them is God.

Though it may not seem so grammatically, the major thrust of this section is directed at the Father. If we want to merge our prayers into Mary's, *we* must first really be *making* those prayers and they must be directed to God. Just as the second section (blessing, praise of Christ) makes no sense unless we think of Christ, so this section makes no sense unless we are awaiting and seeking the Father and his Kingdom.

It is true that the words themselves might permit us a lazier option. We could stop praying to God and ask Mary, for whatever reason, to take over for us. Perhaps all rosary users have done so at times. But any consistent attempt to use the rosary for real meditation will be scuttled by such an approach. The heart and mind raise themselves to God, with longing and a sense of their own inadequacy. The plea to Mary gets its whole strength from that *prior* raising, longing, searching, waiting.

The reader may have practical proof of this. If these words are spoken while seeking the Father, keeping oneself aware of Mary (by the simple fact of talking to her), one can often palpably feel the surge that results by thus opening oneself twice-in-one. As one becomes more adept, the proof will become more and more evident.

If we do not look at the persons to whom we talk, they will ordinarily feel that we are not paying sufficient attention to them. But this rule does not apply to peak experiences. If, to use a crude example, I catch sight of flames working along the ridgepole of my home, I will call in a mighty voice for my neighbor to summon the fire department and bring his garden hose. All the while, of course, my gaze will be rooted to the flames. Still, my neighbor will not doubt that I am giving my full energies both to the fire and to him. Unless we treat this section in the same manner (searching for God while talking to Mary), the rosary itself will not be a powerful experience for us.

There is a practical method for helping oneself here. In the first two sections one first greets Mary, then praises Christ to her. The name *Jesus* has made us aware of his presence before God. Then, when beginning the third section, in which the focus on the Father is powerfully renewed, one can physically turn one's eyes in a new direction. This may be simply a matter of closing eyes that have been open or opening eyes that have been closed. I prefer, at the opening of this third section, to lift my eyes to the sky, that great barrier and symbol of the distance of God. If one employs a statue or painting of Mary, one can look *away* from it even as one speaks to "Holy Mary." By this method, our minds will be programmed to attend to two-in-one. (Along the same lines, see the use of bushes, grottoes, and the like, number 20.K, page 55).

I spoke, above, of the way in which God the Spirit, from eternity, has framed words to be spoken through our lips. "Our Father" (see page 33) and "Hail, full of grace" (see page 41) are examples. In the *first* part of the Hail Mary, then, we greeted Mary by slipping into the stream of communication that has eternally issued from the Spirit. Here, in the *third* part, we slip once again into that stream, but now it is the returning tide from us back to the Father.

We seek the Father, and we practice *qawweh,* being aware that God might enter our lives dramatically even as we wait. Indeed, he has already acted in eternity, his will is already being felt in the world, and he may immediately make us feel the touch of his creative love.

But it is rare for God to reveal his will immediately to the meditator. Rather the Father will speak in the unfolding events of the days to come, or under the signs of the liturgy, though we may still mistake his voice. *Baqqesh*, then, is learning how to seek, but it is not seeking and finding simultaneously.

The Father's advancing future, which we seek in this part of the Hail Mary, is a future compatible with the life and teaching of Jesus: a Jesus-shaped future. Recall that we spoke the name *Jesus* immediately before beginning this section (it is the last word of the previous section). We are, in this section, looking back to the Father, while at the same time we are trying to find Jesus with the Father.

There is a further link between the second and third parts of the Hail Mary: it is *because* we follow Christ (in the blessing) that we seek the prayers of Mary (in the cry). If Christ were not our supreme physician, we would not care in the least to have Mary's prayers, for we know that Mary herself is interested only in promoting Christ.

Holy Mary

There is a common idea in the Bible that God is surrounded by a court of the Holy Ones. Further, when God goes anywhere (into our lives, for example) his Holy Ones come with him (see Zechariah 14:5). In the third part of the Hail Mary, we seek, it is true, the Father—but we may be initially more aware of the Holy Ones who accompany him.

Theologians have speculated for centuries on the multitude of intelligent beings (angels) who must already be in the presence of God. We need not pursue such speculations here. Suffice it to say that the Bible delights in showing us that human beings of great insight (prophets) are also members of God's court. Elected during their lifetimes, some prophets are *assumed* (taken up), becoming full-time members of the court after death (Elijah was one, see 2 Kings 2:9–12). In the New Testament era, because it was thought that the prophetic spirit had been poured out on all those who were reborn in Christ, the title of Holy One became applied to all. Ultimately, as deceased Christians began greatly to outnumber the living, the term came to be used only infrequently of the latter; rather, "Holy Ones" was increasingly reserved for those who, like certain prophets of the Old Testament, had "finished the course" and had been taken up to the heavenly court. When Mary is called "holy," then, it is not simply a compliment to her moral excellence. Rather it indicates her membership in the court.

While reaching toward the Father in the third part of the Hail Mary, we talk laterally to Holy Mary. This is entirely appropriate, for God goes forth with his Holy Ones, giving them the task of revealing himself. Like the angels of the Bible, Mary has no mission but to reveal God and her Son (after whom God's advancing future is patterned).

Mother of God

The expression "Mother of God" may require some explanation. Christianity holds that Jesus is the greatest specimen of human nature. He is truly a human being, not some kind of disguise worn by God. But it is held that the existence of Jesus rests not on the sort of created basis that we all enjoy but directly on the uncreated existence of the Word of God (see page 20). Thus everything that Jesus does, even to having a mother and being brought to birth by her, is somehow an act of God.

Where does God embrace our world if not in its best and noblest? But who is best and noblest if not Jesus? But if God fully communicates in the existence of Jesus, he must embrace all that happens to Jesus, even his conception and his history in the womb. And if God *fully* communicates in Jesus, God must offer nothing less than his own eternal being as the fountainhead of Jesus' creaturely existence.

The expression "Mother of God," then, in no way implies that our heavenly Father has a mother! But it does imply that he whom Mary bore was a person whose unity with the divine was so great as to flow from the eternal existence of God.

Once again the original Greek may shed light on our prayer. In Greek, Mary is here called *theotokos*, "God-bearer." The word implies that the person whom Mary enabled to come into this world was himself an act of God. She has even been called "Gate of God." These words do not imply that Mary takes a maternal role in relation to God in his infinite power and majesty, but rather in relation to God's union with humanity at its highest levels.

Like all the words used in rosary prayers, *theotokos*, Mother of God, brings us back to God himself, the central point toward which we reach in meditation.

Us sinners

The expiation of guilt is a human concern that is seldom entirely out of mind, though we are also adept at suppressing it. The Hail Mary here gives us the opportunity to express this concern, just as does the Our Father in its "Forgive us our trespasses."

From the beginning of this book we have been sending greetings into the limitless unknown. The Hail Mary does as much, but Mary, the nearby Listener, is a human being and so is not absolutely unknown. Additionally, the blessing in the Hail Mary is not directed, immediately, to the Father's mysterious Name, Kingdom, and Will, but to another human being, Mary's son. Only gradually do we realize that he is, in flesh, the Name, Kingdom, and Will. Then we are ready for the next Our Father.

18. The Doxology

Begin the study of the doxology by renewing your Waiting/ Seeking as in number 15.

Glory be to the Father, and to the Son,
and to the Holy Spirit,
as it was in the beginning, is now,
and ever shall be, world without end. Amen.

The biblical word *doxa* signifies "glory." If we think of *doxa*, "glory," as being equivalent to honor and praise, we will not be far from its meaning.

The Doxologies, then, give praise, honor, and glory to God, who is recognized to be eternal (in the beginning, now, ever shall be).

There is not room in a book such as this to discuss the reason why God can be said to be Son and Spirit as well as Father, though these ideas will receive some slight treatment in my discussion of the fifteen mysteries, and in numbers 19 (immediately below) and 25. At the simplest, it may be said that God is praised in the Doxology at the end of each mystery, and that God's praiseworthy presence is detected in experiences of the Son and Spirit. The existence of Jesus is said to rest upon the eternal existence of God-Son (see pages 20, 47, 71).

As a practical matter in meditation, the Doxologies, like so many other aspects of the rosary, simply turn us to the single point, which is God.

19. In the Name (of the Father, and of the Son, and of the Holy Spirit). Amen.

Begin once again with some time spent in Waiting. We have seen above (page 35) that the Divine Name gives access to God. We saw that the blessing of the Name stands near the beginning of the Our Father because the Name is the opening of our relationship to God.

From earliest times, Christians baptized "into the Name" and conducted their meetings "in the Name." Once we have spoken the words *in the Name*, we should proceed with reverence and attention, because God is giving us *his* attention.

Many Christian liturgical acts begin with the phrase "in the Name of (belonging to) the Lord, Amen." Similarly, at the beginning of the rosary, we could well begin with the simple phrase "in the Name. Amen." But, at least from the time when Matthew's Gospel was written, we have gone on to specify that the Name belongs to the Father and also to the Son and Holy Spirit (see Matthew 28:19). All generations of Christians have testified that Jesus (the Son) and the Holy Spirit give access to God in prayer.

They are, in fact, the Name: Jesus is the Name as pronounced in human flesh and blood (for he is a human being), and the Spirit is the Name as pronounced in the invisible but powerful world called Spirit. There is only one Name, and this fact focuses our meditation to one point. Neither the Son nor the Spirit divert us from the One, because the One is the basis on which they rest their existence, the source of their being.

20. Suggestions for the Beginner

[*The following suggestions are intended for the* first *step in rosary meditation: the use of Our Fathers, Hail Marys, and Doxologies*.]

(A)

The full rosary traditionally begins with the Apostles' Creed, to which are added an Our Father, three Hail Marys, and a Doxology (see the diagram on page xviii and prayers on page xix). Those who are using this book merely as a refresher may well precede their meditation with the customary Apostles' Creed. But for the true beginner or for the person who wishes to "go back to the beginning" I recommend that the creed be set aside for the present and that one simply say the Our Father and Hail Mary (and perhaps the Doxology) a few times, concentrating on quality, not quantity. This method can be repeated each day or, better, several times each day. One should return frequently to the ideas about the Our Father and Hail Mary that have been sketched above.

(B)

Learn the prayers as given, even with the *thee's* and *thou's*. Later one might wish to use a different translation. But the meditator is forging links to millions of other people who use the rosary in the English language and, at the outset at least, it is important to say the same rosary as they. The new meditator cannot compare notes with others if the same rosary is not used. Then, too, the rosary is in some respects a *discipline* of meditation, and it is not well for the new meditator to be altering things at the very outset!

(C)

Obtain a set of rosary beads and use them. Meditation is not easy for most of us in today's world. Our minds are drawn away to other thoughts more easily than weather vanes turn in the wind. When we move from bead to bead, even the mere touch of a bead stimulates our minds to enter into the accustomed way of meditation. A bead soon becomes like a telegraph key in the fist of an amateur radio operator: it raises the soul to the act of communication. The single beads that precede each group of ten are for the Our Fathers. (Again, consult the chart on page xviii.)

Upon the following ten beads one may say as few Hail Marys as one wishes. (Later, of course, you will be saying all ten.) Do not pass from one bead to the next until you are really ready to begin the next prayer.

Obtain a rosary that fits your hand. In general this means that people with large hands should not try to use a tiny rosary, since the fingers cannot easily grasp one bead at a time.

(D)

Give quality time to the rosary. Eventually you may be able to use the rosary while walking through crowds or standing in line at supermarkets; it will then be good to fill such times with Our Fathers and Hail Marys. But a beginner can acquire bad habits in such situations and, in any case, they are not suitable for *learning* to meditate. Try to get some period of quiet. Resort to a place that is relatively free of distractions. Try to be rested. Avoid being heavy with food.

(E)

Prepare your body and your mind. Get into a position that can help you stay alert without being uncomfortable. Relax your muscles. Breathe more slowly. Think of the fact that you are actually going to address God himself and Mary of Nazareth.

The preparation for prayer is much more important than one might gather from the size of my treatment of the matter here. We must remind ourselves that meditation involves contemplation, the openness to the action of the Real (see pages 25–26). But God's activity is, very often, gentle. Without proper preparation we will not notice it nor even care about it.

Each individual must experiment, finding the preparations best suited to his or her own nature. One feature of the contemporary rebirth of interest in meditation is the large number of recent books that can give us ideas. Do not be afraid to consult books from any and all meditating peoples of the world, particularly as pertain to preparing for meditation. We in the West have forgotten much; we must be prepared to learn.[18] But the immediate preparation for rosary meditation is of course *baqqesh* (see section J, page 54).

(F)

Even though you are not going to use the Apostles' Creed at this time, do begin your prayer with the formal invocation of God: "In the Name of the Father, and of the Son, and of the Holy Spirit. Amen" (see page 50). If you are a Catholic, or, in any case, do not object, you should trace the cross on your body, using the cross at the head of your rosary for this purpose, while making the invocation. As the Name is our symbol of the whole reality of God, it deserves the fullest attention of which we are capable. Then you are ready to begin the Our Father on one of the isolated beads.

(G)

Should you pray aloud? Yes, if you are not too self-conscious and no one within hearing objects. The audible voice is important,

---

[18] Among those books that proved helpful to me were Mark Link's *You: Prayer for Beginners and Those Who Have Forgotten How* (Niles, Ill.: Argus Communications, 1976), especially pages 7–29, and Bernard Basset's *Let's Start Praying Again.*

for it enters our ears and disposes us to meditation. If you cannot, for whatever reason, pray aloud, then whisper, or at least form the words silently within your mind.

It is true that, in our American culture, few people pray the rosary aloud; you will soon learn to use "silent words" with some effectiveness. But the beginner should not underestimate the power of real speech. The silent places in rosary meditation (also important) come in the pauses, planned or otherwise.

(H)

Locate God and Mary. In order to summon our powers effectively, they must be directed in a specific direction. We know God is everywhere, but it greatly helps if we *consider* him to be in a specific place or direction. This is not an effort to force God, who is infinite, to be at our disposal. Rather, God is very willing to meet us whenever and wherever we call upon his Name with seriousness. (He is willing to meet us and listen; whether he will make us in any way conscious of his presence is up to him!)

All of this applies to praying to Mary. It may sound ridiculous, but one may address her at any suitable spot: on the mantle, beneath a bush, on a cloud in the sky, or behind a door. Everyone understands that this is simply a device for the concentration of our own powers, or, better, a way of making *us* present. Yet, in another way, we must understand that she is not, for all that, the less present for us *there*.

(I)

Should one make use of sacred art? Pictures of God our Father are relatively rare in religious art for the simple reason that they are rarely helpful. They can often be misleading, which is perhaps why the Israelites were forbidden their use (Exodus 20). Pictures that allow us to think more easily of God may, however, be helpful. Many people prefer pictures of nature's majesty. Of course experiencing outdoor nature itself may be a good way of opening our minds to God, provided it is not distracting.

In the case of Mary, a painting or a statue can help us "locate" her very well. Much depends on the individual work of art. Some are so contrary to our taste, or even so contrary to all good taste, as to make them a hindrance. If the work of art makes praying seem more real, without drawing too much attention to itself, it can be encouraged. But a successful rosary meditator will soon ignore the details of a painting or statue to concentrate on the reality of the person addressed. To this end it is usually more important simply to place Mary, using one's imagination, in a specific direction or place, which one then faces. Beginners will probably find that it is helpful not to vary the place or direction of prayer too often.

Although the Hail Marys are not directed to Christ, they are in praise of Christ, and it may likewise be useful to consider Christ as in a specific place or direction. Because of the timelessness reached by prayer, one may address Christ or Mary at any age or condition of life you find suitable, provided you remember that Christ and (in a somewhat different way) Mary are in a state of glory (eternity).

Whether one uses religious art or relies more simply on "locating" the addressed person in a specific direction or place, the most important consideration is that the *presences* of God, Christ, and Mary are not imaginary. They are real; we have direct access to them.

(J)

Spend some time each day practicing *baqqesh-qawweh,* as in number 15, and, of course, use *baqqesh-qawweh* as your immediate preparation for prayer. In the same way we can practice greeting at any time. (We read that the children of Fatima initially said their rosary with nothing but the greetings "Hail Mary . . . Holy Mary.") Greetings alone have been used and highly recommended for centuries; they may still be found in many prayer books under litanies or ejaculatory prayer.

(K)

Bushes, trees, grottoes, niches, clefts in the rocks, ceilings, walls, skies: meditators know that meditation can be helped or hindered by what they admit through their senses. From prehistoric times they have discovered that it is preferable to admit sights that contain numerous distances at once. In this manner the eye (and after it the mind) is drawn forward but does not rest on any one object. For me, nothing succeeds like a bush, especially a bush in which the stems and branches are not obscured by excessive foliage. A large vase of pussy willow also works well. A living stand of swamp reeds or the crown of a tree in winter is also effective. Not for nothing did our ancestors identify sacred trees, groves, and beckoning bushes! The interior columns of ancient temples were arranged like the trunks of trees receding into the distance. The Bible knows its "cleft in the rock" (1 Kings 19:9; Exodus 33:22), and the rosary has often been associated with grottoes and caves. Statues are recessed into niches.

Well known, of course, are the yard shrines of Catholics. In rural areas, especially, these may resemble (or actually be!) old bathtubs half sunken in the ground. Most often these are prominently displayed, even on the very street, where they could not possibly serve our crowded and noisy civilization for prayer and meditation. Parish priests, too, proudly display their Lourdes grottoes and their statues on or near the street. How empty the forms of a once living prayer can be! It should not be necessary to say that the grotto should be arranged in a hidden place that will quiet and lead the mind, a place where one can pray without exposing one's back to the gaze of the traffic of the street.

At times a blank wall or ceiling is useful. Each draws the eye forward while rendering it slightly out of focus. The open sky or a large cloud bank can have the same effect. All such speak eloquently of the invisibility of God. In rosary meditation (unlike certain other effective methods) we let all such objects dispose our souls for meditation, but we do not take an active interest in them.

If you will forgive me one more personal note in this regard, from childhood I have been fascinated by doors half open. I place eternity in the next room, while the opening of the door makes me know that I might at any moment receive a visit!

(L)

Pauses. It is of the greatest importance that the beginner pause before each step. Perhaps it will help to employ the myth described on pages 33, 40, and 45, in which one consciously opens one's mouth to release the words of greeting given by the Spirit of God: "Our Father," "Hail Mary, full of grace." Then one pauses to gather awareness for the blessing section, or for the cry.

In the case of the Hail Mary, the beginner must actually focus on Christ before praising him to Mary and, in the third section, the beginner must pause to turn to the Father, renewing *baqqesh,* while still speaking to Mary.

(M)

I have mentioned the importance of writing and remembering. From this point on, keep a formal journal of your experiences with the rosary. This should include your estimate of your prayers, thoughts, and inspirations, as well as your methodological discoveries and your difficulties. But the journal should contain notable events in daily life as well, for it is a basic assumption of the rosary that God's language is primarily a language of events. Mark Link's book *You* (see Further Readings on page 172) has suggestions for beginning a journal.

(N)

Make use of *prompters* (immediately following).

21. Basic Prompters

The human mind can become a very flabby instrument. We say thousands of things in life without meaning them. Our will power can gradually evaporate. It is not surprising that even a simple prayer or meditation may take a degree of mental energy that we find very taxing. The purpose of prompters is to help the mind get started.

A prompter consists in saying what you intend to say before you actually say it. For example, before saying "Hail, Mary, full of grace," one may say "I will greet Mary."

Nonsense? Remember when you first tried to hit a softball. People kept telling you to keep your eye on the ball. Why did they find it necessary to keep telling you that? Wasn't it obvious that one must watch the ball? But the human mind (knowing and willing) can be so incredibly flabby! The ball must be watched from the moment it leaves the pitcher's hand, or even before. And this requires attention! As we step up to the plate we must say to ourselves, "Now I will watch the ball." If we do *not* say that, others will soon be saying it to us. If this is true of physical motions, it is also true of internal processes. One cannot sing a melody reliably without being able to hear it first in one's mind. A problem cannot be solved unless it is continually reformulated by the mind.

These prompters are indeed excess baggage, and we will have to be rid of them before we can know deep meditation. But one should not be ashamed to use them in the meanwhile, for however long a time they are required. Even experienced users of the rosary may, especially during times of stress, tiredness, or distraction, return to them willingly. They are perfectly natural, and it is only a courtesy to formulate our intentions before opening our mouths!

It is probably true that, if we were members of a preindustrial culture, we would not need prompters. Children certainly have no need of such things. But our minds have become so analytical that we tend to *think about*, rather than *confront*, reality. Paradoxically, our dilemma may be in part the unwanted side effect of a good thing: the decline of idolatry. Idolaters *feel* the presence of divinity in the statue they have carved with their own hands. When they open their mouths to address their idols they experience no self-consciousness or sense of unreality, for they know that the divine ear is only inches away. Modern Christians know in a theoretical way that God is listening, but they have little immediate experience of this fact and must continually remind themselves of it. This is one function of prompters.

Prompters can take many forms. For the Our Father it is sufficient to say "I will seek my Father," "I will now speak to my Father," or the like. It is often a good idea to insert the greeting "Father" at several points in the Our Father.

For the Hail Mary, three prompters are advisable, one for each section of the prayer:

I will greet Mary:	**Hail Mary, full of grace,** etc.
I will praise her son:	**Blessed art thou,** etc.
I will seek my Father:	**Holy Mary, Mother of God,** etc.

When the mind is particularly dull, we may even take the prompters as commands or wishes of Mary herself: "Greet me!" "Praise my son!" "Seek your Father!"

I said on page 53 that we should always pronounce the words of our prayers, silently if not aloud. But the opposite pertains to prompters. While we *may* pronounce them aloud as needed, this is not our goal. The prompters, rather, are designed eventually to be discarded. There will be times when we will not need even to formulate them in mental words. This is because the prompters are *intentions,* and the formulation of an intention is complete as soon as we will to act. The naked intention, unclothed with words, makes itself felt.

But while our goal is to outgrow the prompters, this may not quickly become a permanent achievement. We may often need to pronounce the prompters carefully, allowing their meaning to sink in, or risk running through the words of the prayers without investing a dime's worth of meaning in them.

Many of us who drive automobiles have had the frightening experience of driving for an hour or more and retaining absolutely no memory of the trip, so busy were we with other thoughts. We probably drove with sufficient care, but we cannot remember having done so, and there is a nagging feeling that we may have been careless. While we may be lucky enough to drive safely and absent-mindedly at the same time, there is no such thing as saying the rosary effectively and absent-mindedly. It is the prompters that help us keep our minds on the rosary. This is not to say an inattentive rosary is wasted, but it is far from the ideal.

22. Distractions

Only a person who tries to meditate knows how easily the human mind and will are drawn off course by apparently trifling interruptions in our thoughts or environment. Distractions are a common source of embarrassment and discouragement. How should they be handled?

The remedy must be carefully designed for each individual. And, since we will probably be our own doctors in this matter, it is essential to have as much self-knowledge as possible. Good spiritual direction (if one can get it!) can prevent faulty prescriptions.

Here I cannot avoid getting personal. When I was an adolescent, I, like many teenagers, suffered somewhat from com-pulsive behavior. If a single Hail Mary was "wasted" by a distraction, I could not easily pass it by. I felt compelled to repeat the Hail Mary. Sometimes my repetition of it would be as useless as its initial utterance, and I might repeat it in vain five or six times. But I would never leave it until it was "right." In the course of an entire rosary, of course, this compulsiveness added greatly to the time expended fruitlessly. I would clearly have done better to stop my rosary altogether and turn to some new source of inspiration. I could have pulled down a book on medieval cathedrals or read a passage from the New Testament or have done someone a kind deed. Any of these remedies would have sent me back to my rosary with renewed strength.

Now that I am far from adolescent compulsiveness (and am, in fact, in a period in which the idealism of youth gives way to leniency), an opposite remedy may be required. I do not play competitive sports, so I am unfamiliar with the great metabolic surges experienced by some of my more athletic friends. But sometimes I do allow myself to get angry with myself over distractions. I arise in prayer, raise my voice, pound my fists together: anything to increase my intensity.

We academics train ourselves to notice analogies. In prayer, even our appropriate thoughts generate analogies, and these beget other analogies, so we are quickly led away from our purpose *even by the good features of meditation*. When this happens, my remedy again differs. Far from trying to quicken my pulse, I quiet down. I say to myself that I have no desire to finish the rosary, but only to finish this one Hail Mary. I am going to enjoy it; to do so I will slow down as much as possible. Once it is finished, however, I find myself looking forward gladly to beginning another. By slowing down I have rediscovered the *person* to whom I speak. The conceptual world, with all its distractions, fades into the background.

A general strategy thus emerges: one should take distractions seriously, never accepting them as inevitable. Various remedies can be tried. On the other hand, we must not take distractions so seriously that they consume us. To be continually distracted is a humbling experience, but a little humility works wonders in our relationships with God, just as it can improve our relationships with people.

It may be well to keep track of distractions in the journal. If a common pattern emerges among them, they may not be quite as trivial as they seem. Perhaps our distractions are trying to tell us something. Perhaps we are being alerted to something that needs facing. Perhaps, indeed, they are, in our case, the voice of God!

23. The Rosary Is Not a Substitute for Bible or Sacraments

The mysteries of the rosary are based on biblical scenes, but the rosary is not a substitute for Bible reading. The method of the rosary focuses on God; the details of the mysteries (chapters 4 and

5) do not take us through the very words of an inspired text. In Bible reading, on the other hand, the spoken word, in a thousand artistic and dramatic forms, feeds our soul directly. (See number 35, page 105, "Biblical Studies and the Mysteries.")

Again, the rosary was never meant to replace the Liturgy of the Hours, the Eucharist, or the other sacraments. The reason is simple: the Eucharist (the word is Greek, signifying "thanksgiving") is Christianity's main expression of gratitude, and the Liturgy of the Hours is the continuation of liturgical gratitude around the clock. And while the rosary may generate intense feelings of gratitude within us, it gives us little opportunity for expressing that gratitude.

It has been pointed out that the rosary provides no opportunity to pray *to* Christ. But there is a good reason. The Christian religion provides that union with Christ be chiefly brought about sacramentally, where words are combined with actions, or scripturally, where we have words and actions described. The rosary uses words and intentions without actions.

Never would I wish to encourage the recitation of the rosary during the Eucharist. But the rosary can be an excellent preparation for the Eucharist and a suitable meditation for its conclusion. This subject will have to be postponed until page 148, after my treatment of the mysteries.

On the other hand, nothing I have said here reduces the importance of the rosary. Not only is the rosary wonderfully complemented by the sacraments, the Liturgy of the Hours, and the Bible, it also has something that none of them has. It is the journey of the soul through intensive meditation. There were a thousand years of Christian history when the rosary that we know did not exist. But there has never been a time when human beings were not invited to the rosary's manner of walking with God.

3

The Prayers in Greater Depth

24. Mary and the Our Father

All prayers come from actual praying, so we may safely assume that Jesus derived the Our Father through his own most intimate prayer life with the Father. But it is also true that all of us (and this includes the child Jesus) learn how to pray by bringing to God, for his approval or disapproval, ideas we have learned from our family or civilization.

We know that Jesus' civilization (Israel) gave him many an idea to bring to the Father. I have already said that the ideas of the "prayer of Jesus," the Our Father, can be found in Israel's books of Exodus and Numbers. This fact does not take away Jesus' great originality, because it was only his unique life of personal prayer that enabled him to select those points that are best for our prayer.

If Jesus learned from such sources as Exodus and Numbers, how did the ideas get out of Israelite tradition and into his head? Was it all just a matter of his hearing the Scriptures read, or did various people, such as the rabbis, teach him? Isn't it possible that Mary and Joseph taught the boy Jesus many of the key ideas that he brought to the Father and that reappear in the Our Father?

This suggestion may seem to be a horrifying claim, as though I am trying here to take the spotlight off Jesus and turn it on his parents. But such is not my intention. No matter where Jesus first heard some of his teachings, it was only his own intimate relationship with the Father which, as I have said, gave him the confidence to select the ideal material for prayer. But it should not be surprising that God raised up for Jesus parents capable of teaching him some of the finest achievements of Israelite prayer.

Can it be proved that Mary and Joseph taught Jesus some elements of the Our Father? No, for the New Testament contains no data on this matter. For the purposes of our meditation, however, it helps to understand how the prayer that Jesus taught us fits perfectly the mind of Mary, the person who will join with us in praying the Our Father. And praying the Our Father *with* Mary will increase our confidence in the rosary, Mary's journey to Jesus and the Father.

Everyone can make his or her own list of similarities between the Our Father and the mind of Mary; the following may serve as a beginning.

Our Father who art in heaven, hallowed be thy Name.

Week after week, the most important ritual act of the devout Jewish family is the Sabbath meal. But the Sabbath meal is prepared by the principal woman of the home and it is she who begins the ritual. Lighting candles to signify God's presence, she moves her hands in graceful circles as though gathering in the divine presence itself. She is "hallowing the Name," gathering it into the family, where it will be held in highest reverence. Mary certainly knew what it meant to "hallow the Name."

Thy Kingdom come

All Israelites knew that the Kingdom of God had been revealed on earth through the lives of Moses, David, Ezra, and other great leaders. But most Israelites awaited (*baqqesh*) a still more perfect manifestation of the Kingdom. Messianic expectation, to use our word for it, reached a high pitch at the time of Jesus' birth. Devout

Israelites hoped to hasten the Kingdom by living worthily of it. "Thy kingdom come" was a prayer and a hope on the lips of many in Mary's circle of friends and relatives: Luke, in the first chapter of his Gospel, portrays John the Baptist and his parents, whom he names as relatives of Mary's, as living in the hope of the Kingdom. He depicts Mary herself as one who seeks the Kingdom.

Thy will be done

Devout Israelites knew that God's will had been revealed in the Law of Moses. Although custom decreed that only males made a deep study of the Law, it is a fact that it was most often the women of the house who made it possible for the whole family to revere the Law. The very important regulations covering diet and Sabbath rest, for example, could not be observed without the generous cooperation of the women.

Certainly many Israelite women knew from experience that the most faithful observance of Sabbath, dietary, and other laws was hypocritical if the deeper values of justice and love were not observed. Jesus said, "Nothing that enters a man from outside [such as food] can make him impure; that which comes out of him [malevolence, vices, and crimes], and only that, constitutes impurity" (Mark 7:14–23, from the *New American Bible,* hereafter cited as NAB [Unless the NAB is cited or the quotation is well known, biblical quotations are from my own translations.]). This is a point that many a woman must have instinctively felt as she labored to make a kosher home. In another text, Jesus warns us that minor points of the law, such as having one's wealth declared "corban" (dedicated to God), should not be made excuses for neglecting a parent (Mark 7:10–12).

Give us this day our daily bread

Mary, like other Jewish women, must have taken an interest in women of the Bible. One such was the Widow of Zarephath. Though poor, the widow obeyed the word of God spoken by the prophet Elijah and so risked her tiny store of meal, which was sufficient only for a single day's bread (1 Kings 17:7–24). God rewarded her faith by giving her a supply of grain that was always sufficient for the day. Jesus knew the story well (Luke 4:25–27) and, when formulating the words "give us this day our daily bread," may have thought not only of the Widow of Zarephath but also of a similar widow, his own mother.

Forgive us our trespasses as we forgive those who trespass against us.

The great Old Testament prophet of family life, Hosea, knew from personal experience how mutual forbearance is needed in the family circle. Hosea, in fact, specifically compared family love with the love that God has for Israel. It would be wrong to think that the family of Jesus, Mary, and Joseph had no need to practice *any* sort of mutual forbearance: it was exactly because of the great love in that home that they could practice it easily and to the full.

Lead us not into temptation, but deliver us from evil.

In the days of Jesus' childhood, as I have said, Israel expected a definitive inauguration of the Kingdom of God. This Kingdom would vindicate those good people who, during recent persecutions of the Jews, had given their lives in the cause of God. The advent of the Kingdom, then, would not be an occasion of untroubled peace. It would be a day of justice and calamity for some. The boy Jesus had certainly heard of, and probably seen, the victims of persecutions who had been crucified in Galilee. He came to know how high the stakes really were. We are probably not far from the mark if we imagine Mary discussing these matters with her son. He would later teach us all to pray for deliverance from the great trial (temptation) and its evils.

25. Mary as Patron (Sponsor)

Something wonderful is happening in the Catholic Church and among other Christians too: we are becoming more serious about our sponsors for baptism (godparents). Only a few short years ago people with a child to be baptized often looked down their list of relatives to select the person who would be most offended if overlooked, whether or not that person was devout, upright, or otherwise suited to be a godparent.

Then came the lay movements, such as Cursillo and Marriage Encounter, which insist that candidates have serious sponsors. From these we learned that adult candidates for baptism (Rite of Christian Initiation for Adults) should also have generous sponsors. We now attend classes with the person we are sponsoring; we take part in the various rituals of the catechumenate; we share the joy of the baptism; we accompany the baptized to reunions and postbaptismal mystagogy; through it all we are their Listeners. As she does so often, the Church has taken a page from her ancient history, when baptism was taken very seriously (since, for one thing, it could make the candidate vulnerable to persecution and martyrdom).

In private prayer, when others cannot rush to our side, we still have need of sponsors. God wishes to have us grow not as loners but as people in relationships with others, even if sponsors in the usual sense are unavailable. For private prayer, the Church proposes to us the names of sponsors who have gone before us: the list is called the "canon of the saints" ("Holy Ones," members of God's court, see pages 46–47). We need never pray in isolation; indeed the dead seem especially available!

For the rosary (a private prayer), our patron is Mary. She stands beside us when, like the publican in the Gospel (Luke 18:9–14), we feel unworthy to raise our eyes. She encourages us to speak.

We can certainly go to Jesus alone, but John's Gospel, to name just one source, delights in showing us how to seek a sponsor to take us to him. John the Baptist points Jesus out (John 1:29); Andrew is sponsor to Peter (John 1:41); Philip is the sponsor of Nathaniel (John 1:45) and, later, of some Greeks (John 12:20). In the same Gospel, Mary sponsors the cause of the bridegroom of Cana (John 2:1–12) and becomes the mother of the "beloved disciple" (John 19:26–27).

Even people who have turned from God and have not been able or willing to become fully reconciled to God as they understand him, can stand near Mary as they muster whatever it takes to return to the Father. She desires other Christs, and she will seek them out in places some would consider unlikely.

The notion of "patron saints" is sometimes ridiculed by those who imagine that simple people are more interested in having their favorite patrons than in meeting God. "Patron," indeed, is becoming an obsolete word; the word "patronize" now has unpleasant connotations. But a patron is simply a sponsor, and we have great need of them.

In many religions there are masters who introduce the untrained into the most effective methods of meditation. In Christianity, Christ is the only Master in that sense; all learn from him. The role of Sponsor is less exalted, but is necessary all the same. For this, Mary is ideal.

We pray to God, but we "tell our prayers" to her who has been appointed Listener and mother of every beloved disciple.

26. Jesus and the Absent Father

In Jesus' day there was a special relationship between a firstborn (eldest) son and an absent father. The firstborn son (or daughter, if a son was unavailable) was trained to manage the family farm or business and to take charge when the father was absent, ill, or deceased. As death approached, the father prepared his tomb (people believed that the dead survive in their tombs) and drew up a list of rules for its upkeep. The son would be required to visit the tomb frequently, there to commune with his father. If the son continued to run the farm or business in accord with his father's will, then the father would release blessings, revelations, and his spiritual energy for his son. In that case, the farm or business would prosper still further.

Jesus regarded God as his Father. Although the Father is not dead, he is invisible, just as though he were absent. Jesus, then, behaved toward the Father as would a firstborn son—which in fact he was. Jesus took great interest in God's farm (the whole world, the Kingdom of God). Jesus lived to do the Father's will. He spoke constantly with the Father and, at night, he would go away by himself to commune more intimately with him. The Father favored him with blessings, revelations, and the Spirit. Jesus was, in fact, ready to die in pursuit of the Father's concerns.

But what, in Jesus' day, was done if the firstborn son should die? If the dying son had children of his own, he would have been preparing one to be the new Son or, in some cases, Daughter. If, as rarely happened, the dying son had no children, then the stewardship of the family enterprise would pass to one of the son's brothers. Sometimes the dying son would make the selection, informing his mother of the choice. But in royal families, at least, we know of cases in which the mother made the selection, choosing one of her surviving children to replace her dying son.

When Jesus was dying, according to John's Gospel, he selected someone to be the next "firstborn son." "Seeing his mother there with the disciple whom he loved [the "Beloved Disciple"], Jesus said to his mother, 'Woman, there is your son.' In turn he said to the disciple, 'There is your mother.' From that hour onward, the disciple took her into his care" (John 19: 25–27).

The Gospel seems to be saying that Jesus selects anyone who is his faithful disciple to inherit the Kingdom and his own role as child of God. We notice, too, that Mary's motherhood continues.

It would be just as well not to read this account very literally. But we do know that the Church, from earliest times, has had godmothers: women who, at baptisms, welcome the newly designated sons or daughters of God. Godmothers represent the Church itself, the bride of God, which begets new children for him at baptism, then nourishes and educates them. More than once the New Testament tells us of the new children of this mother (see Revelation 12:17).

Whatever the literal meaning of John 19: 25–27, Mary remains the favorite godmother in the Church. (For Mary as sponsor, see page 67). She wants every Christian to strive, like Jesus, to be fully concerned with God's business. She wants us all to seek to commune with the "absent" Father and to call down his blessing on the business. All new disciples become firstborns, other Christs (Hebrews 12:23).

The rosary, as explained on page 67, is a private devotion; one does not say the rosary in the presence of one's personal godmother. Mary, rather, is the godmother of the rosary. She stands beside you and listens as you praise her first firstborn. She takes up your prayers. She encourages you, ten times in each mystery, to pray devoutly to the absent Father of her Son. Jesus, just as he once acknowledged the Beloved Disciple, acknowledges you as his disciple and "joint heir" with him.

There is something special about the word we translate as "blessed." In the original Greek of the New Testament the word is *eulogomenos*, which is related to our word *eulogy* ("good words": *eu* means "good;" *logos* means "word").

The ancients *eulogized* (blessed) a deceased person. Hearing himself or herself *blessed* with *good words* (eulogy), the deceased person drew near in spirit and (in accord with the Hebrew concept of blessing) reciprocated with "good words" (blessing) for the living.

In the Hail Mary, Mary listens while we eulogize her deceased son ("Blessed art thou among women and blessed is the fruit of thy womb, Jesus"). Jesus blesses us in turn as we ask Mary to pray for us *now* and at the hour when we too enter the world to come.

27. The Trinity as a Unitive Principle in the Hail Mary

God is One, but clearly there are various experiences of him, experiences that Christians generally reduce to three. Christian orthodoxy teaches that the threefold experience is not simply something that happens in *us* but corresponds to a threefold reality in God. In this book, however, I cannot—indeed must not—go off into a defense of the Christian view. It will be sufficient here to show how the rosary, and especially the Hail Mary, deals with this Trinity in the area of our experience. Far too many Christians and Catholics talk confidently (overconfidently?) about what goes on in God, without noticing what goes on in us. Since I am discussing human meditation (what goes on in us) here, I can be forgiven for speaking, at times, without perfect theological precision.

God is experienced as Father, Son, and Spirit (see pages 18–20, 49–50). The whole God makes himself available in each of these, yet there are differences. Because I wish to speak of the differences, which are unified in the Hail Mary, I must suggest, at this point, some rather uncommon terminology: I will speak, just for the moment, of the Indefinite, the Definite, and the Ultra-Definite.

Jesus of Nazareth, a human being, is here considered to be the Name of God as pronounced in flesh and blood. He is very definite. He came from a definite town, lived at a definite time, and was the product of a definite civilization. More importantly, he gave us a clear and definite *example* of how we should live, and he gave us corresponding teachings, which were definite. He did definite deeds of love, including dying on a definite spring day on a horribly definite cross, to the grief of one particular mother.

But even before anyone had found God's Name in Jesus, people had been experiencing a definite side of God. God had revealed himself in the beauty and design of a definite universe. He had done many specific and definite things in human history (the Exodus is the best example in our tradition). God, further, had ways of teaching rather clear principles of morality: from the exploits of Abraham, Moses, Ruth, and others, as narrated in the Bible, people could form definite conclusions about acceptable human behavior. These were supported by the clear and ringing words of the prophets and by very definite commandments such as "Thou shalt not kill!" God had also endowed other nations with reason and touches of the Spirit, and these nations had also acknowledged certain definite models and teachings, which resembled those of Israel.

So we say not only that Jesus is the Name of God pronounced in human nature, but that, in Jesus, God *the Definite* has extended his Uncreated Being. It sounds much better, of course, to say that, in Jesus the Son, God has extended his Uncreated Being, for God is Parent, and parents can have no more definite form of expression than that which comes from them in the form of a child.

But what, then, is the Holy Spirit? We Catholics (and doubtless other Christians) often try to treat the Holy Spirit the same way we treat the Son. We try to picture something definite (a dove, perhaps, or a tongue of flame; see Acts 2). We then try to clothe that definite object with good qualities (wisdom, love, power, and the like) so that we can follow the Holy Spirit as a model, much the way we follow Jesus. Our way of relating to God the Spirit, then, does not differ much from our way of relating to Jesus. The Spirit's *own* way of being experienced is lost in the process.

The Spirit of God is *indefinite,* by which I mean that God is full of infinite variety. I will use a very crude example: when we drive into a filling station for a tank of gasoline, we do not expect to find a different pump for each destination. We do not say "fill it up with California gas, for we are going to San Francisco." Similarly, God gives power that can take us to a variety of destinations. It is Indefinite Power. When, on the other hand, we wish to choose a definite destination, we look to Jesus, the incarnation of the Name of God Definite.

Catholics often feel guilty for "neglecting" the Holy Spirit. We ought to stop feeling guilty. God the Holy Spirit does not expect to get exactly the same sort of recognition that is accorded God the Son. The way to honor the Spirit is simply to *rely* on the Spirit's power. It is not a model, nor a definite goal, and we do not even have to talk to the Spirit. (Notice that traditional prayers to the Spirit are very simple, being mainly pleas for his presence: "Come! Abide! Enkindle!")

Readers will want evidence for this claim. Perhaps the best that can be given is the word *spirit* itself. In all the ancient languages, *spirit* is simply the word for wind. (Even our word *ghost* is related to the word *gust.*) Winds are very indefinite. You cannot see them or know whence they have come nor whither they will blow. Yet they have great power. Not only can they move trees, ships, and people, but they carry seeds and enlivening rain. When mixed with tongues of fire they are quite beyond human control—which is appropriate, certainly, for God.

In the Bible, God's Spirit is associated with anything surprising, anything that comes "out of nowhere." When prophets surprise themselves by their own wisdom, they give thanks to the Spirit. When martyrs are surprised by their own courage, they praise the Spirit. When a person grown rigid in evil suddenly melts, we thank the Spirit. Recall that Jesus is represented as invoking the Spirit before giving his disciples the ministry of reconciliation (John 20:21–22), and he promised that his baptism for the forgiveness of sins would be a baptism of Fire and Wind ("fire and the Spirit"). When new life springs into old bones, the Spirit is recognized (Ezekiel 37). The gifts of the Spirit are a riot of possibilities (Isaiah 11:2–3; 1 Corinthians 12–14). The surprising conception of the Son of God is credited to the Spirit (Luke 1:35), and the regeneration of every Christian has the same cause (Romans 8:14–17). And, last but not least, the power of love (which can truly take us anywhere) is said to be a gift of the Spirit. St. Paul, in fact, tells us that love is the greatest of the gifts of the Spirit (1 Corinthians 13 together with 14:1).

The mystery of the Father

God is infinite. No matter how much he loves us, he is beyond our power to manipulate. God is *ultradefinite,* if I can be forgiven a garish expression which I will not use again! He is beyond ("ultra") any rope we might try to toss over him. He alone has total freedom.

The heavenly Father is said to be "in heaven," because he is, like the sky, beyond us. He loves us, which is why he reaches us through the Definite (Son) and Indefinite (Spirit), without losing his own infinitude.

We human beings have powers corresponding to the three dimensions of God. We have the power to let ourselves be propelled by the Indefinite. We can adapt to the Definite. We can *seek* the infinitely "Ultra," detecting his love, though his glory remains unseen. These three powers are united in rosary meditation.[20]

How does the Hail Mary act as a unitive principle?

Let us now say the Hail Mary again, noticing that, by so doing, we move into threefold unity:

Hail Mary, full of grace, the Lord is with thee.

Before we even begin a Hail Mary, we are seeking (*baqqesh*) the Father: we have just prayed the Our Father, or, more likely, have just finished a Hail Mary whose final section consists in seeking the Father. Our goal, of course, is to keep sight of the Father, watching and waiting, through every subsequent Hail Mary. But as we begin our Hail Mary, at the moment when we are preparing to let God's word of greeting escape from our lips, we notice something that differs, slightly but significantly, from the previous focus on the Father.

It comes with the word *hail* itself. In Luke's original Greek it meant "rejoice in favor." Biblical scholars assure us that one of Luke's great themes is "joy in the Spirit." No gospel writer mentions joy so often as does Luke, and Luke believed joy to be a sign of the presence of the Spirit.

The next phrase, "full of grace (favor)," also suggests the Spirit, for God's favor is always a surprise, always uncontrollable. Even our Christian word *grace* is usually attributed to the Spirit. These opening words, too, are taken from Luke's story of the conception of Jesus, in which the Holy Spirit comes down upon Mary.

Luke often speaks of praying "in the Spirit." The Wind that carried Mary's good news to her was the Spirit, and the Wind that carries our greeting to her is also the Spirit.

---

[20] This is not surprising, for if we accept the analysis of Karl Rahner, the best model for thinking about the Trinity is that of communication in which three elements can be observed. Rosary meditation, as I have said, is founded on the act of communication. See Rahner's *The Trinity* (New York: Herder and Herder, 1969).

The Spirit is the power that touches every sinner, prompting conversion. No person on earth is totally divorced from the Spirit. Any of us, then, can be heard by Mary, if we address her with these words, which themselves imply addressing her "in the Spirit." (We can even modify our first prompter in each Hail Mary as follows: "I will greet Mary in the Spirit.")

Words, of course, are not our salvation. The important thing is not simply to pronounce these words, as though they were magic, but to fall back trustingly into the gale that blows from God. Let us fill our sails with the Holy Spirit. And the nature of human beings is such that the mere act of *trying* to trust God is already to trust, is already "letting go."

The Holy Spirit is speaking to Mary–the people. There is an infinite "Hail Mary, full of grace" being spoken through the universe from the timelessness of God. Mary became aware of it two thousand years ago, but, in the world of God, there are no limitations imposed by time. Thus, when we begin the Hail Mary, we are simply deciding to open our wills so that the divine word can move through us, becoming ours, to some extent, as it moves. By beginning the Hail Mary we are choosing God Indefinite. We can place no limits on where he my bear us. He may even generate a new child of God in us!

Blessed art thou among women and blessed is the fruit of thy womb, Jesus.

Here we narrow our focus from the Indefinite to the Definite. In this section, we praise the definite in Jesus Christ, which implies that we pause an instant to "see" Jesus. Doubtless we will see Jesus in a variety of ways, depending on whether we are thinking of him in glory, in his public mission, or on Mary's lap. Only if we do see something definite about him, however, can we praise him sincerely to Mary. (chapters 4 and 5, on the mysteries of the rosary, teach us to integrate the numerous aspects of Jesus.)

The praise of Jesus, the second portion of the Hail Mary, is the praise of God Definite, for Jesus is God's best idea of a human being. The praise of Jesus is a continuation of our basic thrust to the Father, for Jesus is the Father's word made flesh. We no longer simply rely on the divine power (Spirit), but through praise we continue to reach beyond. And praise is empty unless, little by little, we conform our lives to the life of Jesus, increasingly putting our whole being (morally, spiritually) into this reaching for God.

Holy Mary, Mother of God, pray for us. . . .

In Jesus we have experience of the Definite, but God remains beyond all. We search for the Father, stretching toward him, by merging our prayers into Mary's, which also sweep toward the Father. And the power by which Mary's (the people's) prayers sweep back to the Father is the power of the Spirit (see page 45).

We cannot "see" the Father. It is true that, if we have seen Jesus, we know we are aiming in the right direction. We will know the Father by his love. But the Father is invisible, beyond, free. In him we are reminded of the limitless unknown.

Each Hail Mary, then, helps us know and unify the threefold experience of God. In turn, our own "three-ness" (definite, indefinite, mystery) is unified. All of this may seem, perhaps, tenuous and fleeting. But it is the repetition of the Hail Mary that allows us, layer after to layer, to build up these experiences, strengthening them, giving us Communication.

28. Poverty of Spirit and the Prayers

It is well known that, at the time of Jesus, the faithful of Israel, or at least certain groups of them, called themselves *the poor*; there was an understanding that God comes to the aid of his "poor." The poor-rich contrast, however, had a clear reference to the life of prayer and meditation: God, the Giver of Life, would visit those in prayer who had made room for him, divesting themselves of inner resources developed apart from him. Jesus himself gave powerful support to this tradition, cautioning his disciples that only the "poor" (Matthew 5:3) would be open to the Kingdom of God.

Already in the spirituality of the Psalms we learn that the method of *baqqesh,* in which we fasten our eyes expectantly on God, relying on no other supports, is answered by deep spiritual joy.[21] It is not surprising that Luke, a New Testament champion of *baqqesh,* has also woven the themes of spiritual poverty and consequent joy in his Gospel.[22]

There is nothing very complicated about this: when we seek, we look to the future, and the future is *entirely* beyond us. We have nothing of its benefits until it arrives. It is the same with *greeting,* the simple act upon which rosary meditation is built: a greeting is all possibility. One never knows what response it will bring. It is essential poverty, because it passes all the options over to the person greeted. And the most surprising of all partners in communication is God. Those who seek and those who greet make themselves poor, but potentially rich. Putting it still more simply: the poor are always the best seekers.

The unknown author of *The Cloud of Unknowing* teaches us the importance of jettisoning everything, burying all beneath a "cloud of forgetting." Even our elaborated world of concepts must be left behind. We seek the direct intuition that God is good and we are only "sin." (In calling us "sin," the author aims at a meditative technique, not a balanced theological statement.) But the author also understands that there is a poverty on the level of being, an intuition of our dependency in being, our opening to the self-existent being of God. We are taught a technique for giving up our self-centered awareness of our own being.

The technique of Zen meditation differs in that its intuition of being is sought in concrete, existing objects. Still, Zen, like *The Cloud,* "seeks to awaken a direct metaphysical consciousness beyond the empirical, reflecting, knowing, willing and talking ego. . . ."[23] Indeed there are many routes to a direct intuition of

---

[21] Psalm 4:7 is typical: "Lord, you have given more joy to my mind than others have known, for all their grain and their wine."

[22] The Canticle of Mary (Luke 1:46–55, see page 153–54) begins: "My soul proclaims the greatness of the Lord, my spirit rejoices in God my Savior, for he has noticed the poverty of his handmaid."

[23] Thomas Merton, *Zen and the Birds of Appetite* (Gethsemane, Ky.: Abbey of Gethsemane, 1968), page 49.

being as encountered in particular beings, but all methods, by putting us directly in touch with actual being, make us know its radical dependencies and its intimate ties to the Self-existent.

Rosary meditation is equally effective here. We recall that the Our Father makes us aware of being *receivers*, beneficiaries of a Name/Kingdom/Will that is being extended to us and shaping us as the human race. But the objects we confront in rosary *baqqesh* are rather segments of time than of space: we are searching, awaiting *events* in the approaching future. (Events are ordinarily underappreciated because, apart from meditation, they are seldom the objects of much search; they have not been awaited.) Again, coming events are entirely beyond us, and greeting passes all the options to the other. Finally, there is the recognition that it is the radical poverty of our own language of events that qualifies us to be taught a new language of events from God.

All these workings of the rosary will appear more clearly when we enter the mysteries in the next chapter. Yet we should not be anxious to hurry on. The rosary without the mysteries is already a wonderful path of meditation. The mysteries too, as Luke already conceived them, are a universe of meditation. But to integrate the two successfully, thus attaining the unique and powerful form of meditation called the rosary, requires a solid foundation in the prayers.

Questions for the journal:

Are you now more respectful, more genuine, more truly present when you greet other persons? Are you now more grateful for time? Do even objects of nature and art seem to have more selfhood? Do you begin to perceive that events exist in abeyance, awaiting the best participants?

4

A First Look at the Mysteries

29. Enumeration of the Mysteries

The mysteries are fifteen scenes in the life of Jesus. These scenes have the ability to call forth powers from deep within us and to open us to divine communication. With the powers thus summoned we more deeply penetrate the real, learn better our own dialect of God's language of events, and grow in union with him and with all created being. Because they are scenes in the life of Christ and, very often, Mary, they help us better to appreciate those two persons and, consequently, God himself. Because these scenes proved to have unforseen power, they are fittingly called "mysteries," a Greek term (*mystēria*) meaning "hidden things."

As explained on page 7, the meditative method of the rosary consists in having us concentrate (raise) our powers of knowing and loving to a single point, which is the *person* to whom we pray. The mysteries help us to *know* the person to whom we pray (ultimately God), and they do this in a way that is largely intuitive and unanalytical.

The fifteen mysteries are divided into three chaplets, each containing five mysteries. The three chaplets are designated as the joyful mysteries, the sorrowful mysteries, and the glorious mysteries. Their traditional names are:

The Joyful Mysteries

The Annunciation
The Visitation
The Nativity
The Presentation
The Finding of the Child Jesus in the Temple

The Sorrowful Mysteries

The Agony in the Garden
The Scourging
The Crowning with Thorns
The Way of the Cross
The Death of Jesus

The Glorious Mysteries

The Resurrection
The Ascension
The Descent of the Holy Spirit
The Assumption
The Crowning of Mary

30. The Simple Humanity of the Mysteries

The list of the mysteries given above may seem very theological, especially given the Latin titles (Annunciation, Visitation, etc.), which so many of them have. But there is also a simple human scene that is at the core of each mystery. This may be illustrated by the following list in which a new title or caption to each mystery is given. In each mystery, the title attempts to capture not just what happened to Jesus and Mary, but something we can all experience.

The Joyful Mysteries

1. A mother is expectant for the first time. Her hopes are boundless! *(Annunciation)*
2. Two expectant mothers meet. The younger, as sometimes happens, is a blessing to the older. *(Visitation)*
3. An infant, even in the poorest circumstances, captures all hearts. *(Nativity)*
4. A needy world stakes out its claim on a baby. *(Presentation)*
5. Every child gets occasional glimpses of its duty to others. *(The Finding of the Child in the Temple)*

The Sorrowful Mysteries

6. No matter how well loved, a human must face death alone. *(Agony in the Garden)*
7. When in great pain we are necessarily alone. *(The Scourging)*
8. In humiliation we are uniquely alone. *(The Crowning with Thorns)*
9. The machinery of death overtakes each of us separately. *(The Way of the Cross)*
10. In death we live out our total dependency. *(The Death of Jesus)*

The Glorious Mysteries

11. In searching for a loved one we acquire the hope of reunion. *(Resurrection)*
12. The dead one is lost to sight; the living one returns to duties. *(Ascension)*
13. Soon the Spirit of God touches the living one; she rejoices, knowing it is the absent one who sends the Gift. *(The Descent of the Holy Spirit)*
14. The one who is alone feels the need to be taken to a place of protection on the wings of God. *(Assumption)*
15. The one who grows old can hope to be allowed to serve even after death. *(The Crowning of Mary)*

These "human" titles are not meant to abolish the supernatural character of the mysteries in favor of the human alone. But the human aspect of the mysteries can touch us deeply (since we are human), energizing our meditation. One may pass a theology exam without noticing the human element, but that would not be much use for meditation. (The reader may quickly improve on my expressions of the human element in the mysteries.)

31. Miracles in the Mysteries: A Challenge to Faith?

A glance at the preceding table of mysteries shows that several, notably the Resurrection and the Annunciation (which includes the virginal conception of Jesus), involve events generally considered miraculous. Here is a matter passed over in silence in number 11 ("Does one have to be a Catholic to use the Rosary?"). Clearly most non-Christians, and even some Christians, do not accept the miracles as historical events. While a person who doubts the miraculous elements in the mysteries may still find them helpful for rosary meditation, a closer look at the problem may prove fruitful.

Some Catholic readers may be growing impatient. Why not get on and finish the book for those who can use it (presumably Catholics) without standing the whole thing on its head to include others?

The miraculous, however, is a problem for many in our society, both within and without the Catholic Church. Some who most vehemently protest their faith in the miraculous often do so while unconsciously altering the very meaning of the miracles they supposedly accept. Everyone knows Catholics who insist, rightly enough, on the physical resurrection but have no patience with Bible passages that describe the resurrection in spiritual terms. These "brave" believers scrupulously garner every shred of evidence for the physical side of the resurrection, as though that event were identical to what emergency medical teams often achieve: a resuscitation. If they could find the medical records of an attendant postresurrection physician they would consider the resurrection proved well enough to satisfy any critic. But they also ignore the *consequences* of the resurrection, its meaning in the realm of the spirit.

Thus there is a need to introduce the miraculous in a new context, one that will fit this subject—meditation—however inadequate it may be for the various branches of theology. In so doing I may succeed in easing certain difficulties, while simultaneously uncovering the real and deeper challenges of meditation.

From the meditator's point of view, many of the problems we have with miracles stem from the stale popular science that we have all absorbed. The most up-to-date science of our times is not unfriendly to rosary meditation. Yet most people are still catching up with the science of the nineteenth century, a type of science that was decidedly against the idea of miracles.

Nineteenth-century science, which was the perfection of Newtonian physics, saw most reality as a collection of microscopic particles. The scientist's role was chiefly to measure the masses, velocities, and charges of these particles and, from the data collected, to describe and know, potentially, everything. For those who had the measurements, reality was cut and dried: definite, inevitable, and predictable. There was no room for anything miraculous.

Science is now learning that basic material reality is mysterious and unpredictable. Its roots are not stable; rather they are ready for anything! Scientists are saying that material reality actually seems ready to reveal itself in different forms, depending on the kinds of experiments investigators devise in their searchings. Thus subatomic realities are correctly said to be particles, but they can also reveal themselves to be waves (like ripples in a pond, something very different), depending only on the way we investigate them.

Scientists further say that subatomic realities are too fluid to have, simultaneously, both locations and velocities (two quite different things), but that the choice, again, depends on how we seek them. (Imagine air traffic controllers trying to deal with airplanes that could be located *or* tracked, but not both.) It is not just that basic matter is hard to study: rather it is so incredibly plastic that we can say with literal truth that the universe we seek is the universe we find. Nor are scientists saying that our grasp on reality is purely subjective: rather the indeterminacy of basic matter is an objective fact in the world outside the mind.

Computer scientists have learned to create data banks that can copy themselves with all needed variants as often as they are searched by operators with special sets of assumptions. But physics describes the universe itself as a giant program that is so flexible that it can reproduce itself with variants depending on how it is searched. But if such a secondary universe were called up often enough, could it not become primary? Would it not have "arrived?"[24]

This is what theologians have always said. In the real world, there is always hope. The reality we seek is actually out there somewhere; it may well get on our time-line and move down toward our present, if only we know how to search for it. Theologians who specialize in questions of morality have likewise pointed out that the universe we want is the universe we get. (An unkind person is soon surrounded by unkindness.) Now we see that this applies to every aspect of reality.

It is still taught in schools that fires erupt when certain molecular particles collide, and wars break out when certain nations collide. This way of thinking assumes that events are reactions of particles (small scale or large scale), that particles are prior to events. But physics now sees events (energy operating over time) as prior to the things that participate in them. Events, at least at the microcosmic level, make their own "particles" as needed so that things may "happen" on that level. Microcosmic reality is so indeterminate that it must be shaped into pools of greater determinacy (we call these "particles") in order that an event may occur there!

---

[24] For the multiplicity of worlds as a feature of quantum physics see "Many Worlds," chapter 11 in John Gribbin's *In Search of Schrödinger's Cat: Quantum Physics and Reality* (London: Bantam Books, 1984).

There is resistance to applying these insights to the larger world, and no wonder! If events are prior to the individuals and peoples who participate in them, then perhaps events are words of God that can be summoned by *baqqesh*! If human bodies were as "ready for anything" as smaller bodies are, then how could we rule out new states of being (such resurrection) or new ways of becoming real (such as virginal conception)?

No mere book about meditation will convince the reader for whom these ideas are new. Even a rear guard of scientists has, quite properly, been resisting them throughout most of the twentieth century. For the uninitiated reader it will suffice, perhaps, merely to realize that science's old "clear and definite" view of basic reality is no longer confidently taught by scientists.

The value of the new physics, from the standpoint of meditation, is that it admits the possibility of radically new things in the world—things that, in comparison with what has been, are miraculous. This does not imply that the past has no connection with producing the new event; rather the new event has been shaping the "particles" of the past all along.

The Resurrection

Without going further into science, let us see where the new thinking will take us in matters miraculous. "Seek and you shall find," said Jesus (Luke 11:9; Matthew 7:7 [NAB]) and elsewhere (Luke 12:31; Matthew 6:33), "Seek first the Kingdom of God and its justice and all these other things will be added to you." Jesus, in his own *baqqesh*, explored for a resurrected universe and, according to Christians, found what he wanted. The universe shaped itself into the resurrection or, better, had always been able to duplicate itself as a resurrected universe in other space-time coordinates. Jesus searched for the resurrection event and was himself shaped by its approach so that it could "happen" in him. God, to speak more theologically, had always decreed a resurrected universe but could not reveal it until (and then only in a limited way) some one individual searched for it with sufficient hope (see number 6).

What was the resurrection for which Jesus sought? By comparing numerous biblical passages, reading them against the background of other literature of his day, we can form some idea:[25] Jesus wanted all wrongs to be righted, all innocent sufferers, alive or dead, to be vindicated. Jesus' idea of resurrection, however, was more profound than that of others of his day. For him, resurrection was not a matter of crudely rewarding people with compensatory delights. It was, to use a modern term, the lost *potential* of the victim that Jesus wanted to see redressed. He wanted all legitimate human aspirations and latent powers to be fully developed. It was Jesus' confidence in unimagined potential that fits so nicely with the thrilling vistas now being sketched by science.

Does the rosary user have difficulty (admitted or otherwise) with miracles? I propose a greater challenge. The rosary user should believe that the universe Jesus wanted, embodying his own sophisticated notion of resurrection, actually exists somewhere and, of course, includes Jesus himself.

When Christians hear the possibilities of resurrection denied, they feel a sadness, of course, over the good that is thus lost. In this book, however, the sadness is slightly realigned: the good whose loss we mourn is the loss of the power of *baqqesh*. If someone denies that Jesus, through his *baqqesh*, could have sum-moned the resurrected world, that person is denying the power of *baqqesh* itself, including his or her own power of *baqqesh*.

It is important to stress that, while Jesus sought a general vindication of all sufferers, this has not yet been obtained at our point in time. We would say that it exists somewhere, but that only Jesus has found it. Looking at the matter in this way, we achieve an explanation of the known situation: Jesus' search succeeded because he was a peerless searcher, and the full and general vindication does exist. But here in our space-time coordinates it does not yet exist, because others have not yet sought it sufficiently.

---

[25] David Bryan, *From Bible to Creed* (Wilmington, Del.: Michael Glazier, 1988, distributed by Liturgical Press, Collegeville, Minn.) pages 58–68, 132–45.

The *baqqesh* of Jesus Christ reached its apex as he neared his death. It was in the last twenty-four hours of his life, from his meditation in the Garden of Gethsemane to his very crucifixion, that he rapidly approached that which his pure hope and intense search had been seeking: the resurrection-universe. We cannot even guess at the transformations this produced in his own human nature as the new event made final preparations in him. The New Testament attempts to hint, to nudge us in the right direction. It speaks of Jesus having the power to come and go as he pleased, even the power of bilocation and the power to penetrate "solid" things. When people doubt the resurrection, they are often doubting their own understanding of these New Testament hints. It is well to remember that these are only attempts to put us on the right track. No one of us has experienced the resurrection-universe; none can presume to understand it. Doubters can relax, for even the most assured Christians do not know *firsthand* what they are affirming when they affirm the resurrection. They can only affirm that Jesus entered the marvelous universe that he had always sought.

The Annunciation (virginal conception)

The worldview of the old science (and we all share it to some extent) was particularly hostile to this mystery. The virginal conception of Jesus is not the prime focus of the mystery, yet it is a red flag to those whose thinking is limited by nineteenth-century science. The main problem for them (us?), on examination, can be more accurately stated as this: the Annunciation proclaims that something *new* entered the world. Newtonian physics (like Darwinian biology and Marxist economics) leaves no room for anything radically new. Everything must be no more than an inevitable outgrowth of the interactions of particles (or species or economic classes).

What the Annunciation proclaims is a Second Beginning, a New Genesis. The Gospels of John and Mark both open with the word *archē* ("beginning"), the Greek equivalent for the Hebrew title of the Book of Genesis. Luke's Gospel presents Jesus as a new

Son of God, which is to say, a New Adam. *Baqqesh*, it seems, is far more powerful than even Israel had guessed.

In what did Jesus' radical newness consist? I have already said that Christianity understands that the act of existence that underlies the man Jesus is not a created existence, such as we all enjoy, but rather the uncreated existence of the Eternal Word of God. This sublime idea maintains, then, that Christ is God's Communication, the very thing that rosary meditation is based upon. The Eternal Word theology, however, is first recorded in John's Gospel (John 1:14). Luke puts the matter differently: Jesus, Mary's child, was conceived by the Spirit of God (Luke 1:35), the very Spirit that hovered over the waters of the original creation (Genesis 1:1–2). Matthew's Gospel (1:18–20), written entirely independently of Luke's, agrees.

Let us note that Luke's seemingly preposterous idea fits very well with the newer science. If events are primary and impose their needed determinateness on the indeterminacy of matter, then we cannot say what is impossible just by looking at matter. What we can do is look at our indeterminate world and notice how indeterminate things are stirring into patterns ("particles") under the impress of arriving events. We can even detect "laws of nature" that describe the evolving processes, and with this knowledge we can invent our computers, radios, and medicines. We can help bring to birth amazing improvements in our world, provided we do not declare in advance anything good to be impossible.[26]

Both Luke and Matthew combine the "Spirit conception" of Jesus with the tradition of his virginal conception. Here, too, the newer science can be suggestive. Just as reality, in its relatively indeterminate states, is subject to arriving events, so those arriving events must rearrange (make more determinate) local reality; otherwise events cannot arrive in particular coordinates of spacetime. The ordinary biological patterns associated with concep-

---

[26] That there is nothing impossible to God is the point of Sarah's unexpected pregnancy in Genesis (18:14); Luke quotes this passage in the Annunciation (1:37).

tion, noble as they are, could not have remained unchanged by something as new as conception by the Spirit of God. And Jesus *was* new! People sensed it in the way he settled disputes of the law: with personal authority. They sensed it in the authoritative way in which he rebuked troublesome spirits or, for that matter, fevers. He was the first person to practice the "cult of the absent Father" (see number 26) with God substituted for Joseph, and the first to be recognized as having been a resurrection-man. They had sought the new Israel but had gotten the new Adam. These and many other elements in the arriving Jesus-event argue for something new, a radical break in the usual ways of the world. Why should we hesitate to accept something in his birth narrative that we would not be surprised to find in distant ages of the world?

Jesus was new, the gift of God, but he was also the result of human yearning: Israel's yearning for a new Israel and the world's yearning for a new world (attested, for example, in Virgil's *Fourth Eclogue*). God could not allow a Jesus to walk the earth until a Jesus was, at least implicitly, sufficiently longed for, hoped for.

There were many powerful meditators in Israel at the time of Jesus. The New Testament tells us of Joseph, Elizabeth, Zachary, John the Baptist, Simeon, and many others. The *baqqesh* of these, and of millions of others from the beginning of time, had been gradually focusing, penetrating, becoming one *baqqesh* searching for the new Adam. But Jesus, like everyone else, was to begin life as a child and it was fitting, even necessary, that his mother be the queen of meditators, a peerless vessel of hope, the final lens through which the combined *baqqesh* would achieve its purpose. Thus it is important to realize that, as St. Augustine put it, Mary conceived Jesus in her heart.[27] She embodied all the elements of

---

[27] Anthony Bloom, *Beginning to Pray* (op. cit.), on page 111 quotes a statement of Charles Williams in his *All Hallows Eve*: "... One day a virgin of Israel was capable of pronouncing the sacred name with all her heart, all her mind, all her being, all her body, in such a way that in her the word became flesh."

Israel seeking, just as Jesus embodied all the elements of *Israel found*. Jesus is, in an important way, the Israel-Adam that was hoped for by Mary the virgin.

All human beings derive their materiality from their mothers' bodies; even the words *mother* and *matter* are related (Latin, *mater* and *materia*). But basic matter, "mother matter," we now know is wonderfully open, wonderfully responsive. Thus it was almost inevitable that in the course of human history, somewhere, sometime, the purified longings of the human race, fueled by God's creative love, would send matter into whatever patterns were necessary for the conception-event of the new Adam. And, I contend, the person who put the final focus on all of this was the mother of the child.

Nobody is that great? But Mary focused the longings of all humanity throughout human history. These longings had to emerge somewhere, and, no matter where they burst forth, there would always be people saying the exit point was not worthy enough. In any case, Mary could not, and did not, do it alone. The human race did it.

We can all do as much: if we hope with a hope sufficiently strong and pure, a new child will be enkindled, by God's gift, in that most unlikely matter: ourselves. Israel sought a new Adam; our task is to seek a new Jesus. Only if we have finally despaired of ever becoming the new human beings we desire to be are we really qualified, experientially, to deny the *baqqesh*- conception of Jesus Christ. By the same token, only by having experienced the power of *baqqesh* to remake us can we, authentically, boast of our faith in that conception.

32. A Brief Description of the Mysteries

The reader should read through the description of the fifteen mysteries presented here. But because I recommend that the beginner actually use only the first one or two mysteries for his or her initial trial, the material need not be *learned* as it is read. There will be many opportunities to return to it later.

Because all but two of the mysteries can be found in the writings of Luke, the biblical references for each have been given. These descriptions, however, are highly condensed. There are many details in the biblical texts that, while of the highest importance for the reading of the Bible, would not be helpful to meditation as it is practiced in the rosary. I do not, then, recommend that the biblical passages be read in immediate connection with the rosary, though they should be well known on their own merits. Then too, these descriptions contain, in small measures, some of the meditative fruit that each mystery has produced over the centuries. The beginner might not be able to see these ideas in the biblical texts, at least not at the outset.

The first joyful mystery, the Annunciation, is in some ways the most important—not in the history of Jesus' mission, of course, but as showing forth the assumptions about prayer, hope, *baqqesh*, and meditation, which underlie the entire rosary. The Annunciation, in fact, has given rise to another separate devotion in Latin Catholicism, that called the Angelus.

Because these descriptions are so highly condensed, the reader may be inclined to doubt their effectiveness. Chapter 5 will treat the mysteries in greater depth, but a beginning at meditating must be made on the basis of the condensed descriptions given below. Sheer detail such as that available in chapter 5 would stifle the basic thrust of the meditation.

The Annunciation [*Luke 1:26–38*]

Mary, a maiden of the tiny town of Nazareth, betrothed to a man called Joseph, is one who hopes and searches *(baqqesh)* intensely and unselfishly for the full advent of God's Kingdom (justice, peace, love, fidelity to God) among us. Mary is made aware by angelic perception (more on this following) that she has found favor with God and will give birth to the Messiah, the individual who will inaugurate the divine Kingdom for which she has hoped. She is further made aware that the child to be born will be conceived in her by the Spirit of God; she understands and signifies her readiness. She has also received the knowledge, which serves as a sign that nothing is impossible with God, that an aging kinswoman, Elizabeth, is unexpectedly six months pregnant.

A detailed comparison will show that certain elements in my summary do not come from Luke 1:26–38. The claim that Mary "hopes and searches intensely and unselfishly" for the Kingdom, for example, is based on the entire New Testament portrait of her, and on the very nature of the rosary tradition, whose starting point is that human hope is preliminary to divine activity (see number 6). Similarly, the Bible's texts are sometimes too detailed for the rosary's type of meditation.

Furthermore, such details as I do take from Luke are taken from Luke himself. No effort is made to see behind Luke to the earlier, pre-Lucan, shape of the tradition. Thus the virginal conception of Jesus may have had quite a different narrative function in an earlier stage of the tradition about the Annunciation, but it is Luke's mystery that forms the basis of the meditation.[28]

The remaining mysteries (following) are handled in a similar manner. We see again why the Bible texts, as worded, are not the immediate vehicles of rosary meditation (see number 35, page 106, "Biblical Studies and the Mysteries.")

What is Angelic perception?

Christian theology, like numerous other theologies and philosophies, holds that God has created many beings of a more in-

---

[28] By not going behind Luke to his hypothetical sources, I may appear to be a fundamentalist, showing interest only in Luke's finished scenes, as though their "plain sense" were all that is to be gotten from the passages in question. Rather, I take the view that Luke intended his scenes for meditation and gave them the shape that would best speak the truth of the meditation to the mind of the meditator. This sets *my* policy, however valuable other approaches to the material may be for the simple history of the events narrated.

telligent nature than our own. These are very close to God and are employed by him whenever he wants to help people like us to penetrate mysteries of great depth. Communication, it would seem, is a process in which *all* intelligent beings participate, particularly when the infinite intelligence of God is bending toward the very limited intelligence of human beings. In the Bible, such higher intelligences are called "angels." The Bible describes them graphically and even supplies them with names (such as *Gabriel*, "Power of God," who appears in the annunciation scene of Luke's gospel).

(Quantum physics now indicates that events in one part of the universe can instantly influence events in every other part of the universe. Thus it ought not be surprising that when a human being attempts a great *baqqesh* and succeeds, all other knowing powers in the universe would be connected.)

This is an example of how the picturesque scenes of the Bible may be too detailed to aid meditation. It is more helpful, in the rosary, to focus on the way in which Mary's perceptivity, itself an outgrowth of divine favor, has been enriched by this new contact with the divine, rather than to dwell on the names and speaking styles of angels.

The Visitation [*Luke 1:39–56*]

Mary, bearing in her womb the child who will be called Son of God, visits Elizabeth, not because she doubts the knowledge she has received, but, it would seem, to share her own joy over the coming of the new Israel. (Perhaps, too, she simply understands it to be God's will that she visit her kinswoman.) Elizabeth is full of joy over her own unborn child, whom she believes will be a great prophet (he is, of course, John the Baptist), but she has long been seeking the Kingdom and is able to enter into the wider joy of Mary's news. Greeting Mary at the doorway of her house, she acknowledges the blessing she is receiving by Mary's visit, saying "Blessed art thou among women, and blessed is the fruit of thy womb." She praises Mary's confidence (faith) in God's annunciation and states that the baby in her own womb leapt for joy at the approach of Mary (and her unborn child). Mary then utters her famous *Magnificat* (treated separately on pages 153–54, with the text on page 170).

The Nativity [*Luke 2:1–20*]

Mary and Joseph, now married, go to Bethlehem, the birthplace of Joseph's ancestor, King David, to comply with a Roman edict that all Jewish families must return to their ancestral homes to be enrolled in a census. Because of the crowds returning for the census, the inn has no suitable space for a woman about to give birth. Mary and Joseph seek the solitude of a stable, and Jesus, newly born ("wrapped in swaddling clothes"), has nowhere to be laid except in the animals' manger. Nearby shepherds are aware by angelic perception that a baby newly born in Bethlehem is to be the Messiah and the "joy of the whole people," including even poor shepherds such as themselves. The shepherds expect to recognize the baby by the very striking fact that it is newborn and lies in a manger. The shepherds' *baqqesh* is successful: they arrive and find the child in the manner they have been expecting. They tell what they know, while Mary "treasured all these things and reflected on them in her heart."

The Presentation [*Luke 2:22–40*]

Some weeks after the birth of Jesus, the family goes to the temple in Jerusalem. Jesus, as a firstborn, must be ritually given back ("presented") to God in accordance with the Law of Moses. The parents then offer God two young doves, and God, in accord with the meaning of the ritual, graciously allows the parents to take their child home for the time being. But God has a wonderful mission to entrust to this child who has been presented to him: to the amazement of the parents, a man of Jerusalem named Simeon arrives, blesses the child (by taking him in his arms and blessing God) and declares prophetically that Jesus is not only the glory of Israel but also the "light of the nations." He also says that Jesus will be rejected by many and that a sword will pierce the soul of Mary. An elderly prophet, Anna, confirms what Simeon has said.

The Finding of the Child Jesus in the Temple [*Luke 2:41–52*]

When Jesus is twelve years of age (and thus responsible for keeping the Law of Moses), Mary and Joseph take him to Jerusalem to celebrate the Passover there. After leaving the city, Mary and Joseph discover that Jesus is not, as they supposed, traveling with relatives in the caravan. Returning with great anxiety to Jerusalem, they begin a search (*baqqesh*) for Jesus and, on the third day, they find him at the temple, the house of God. He is conversing with the religious experts, who are amazed at his intelligence and his replies. When Mary, deeply moved, asks Jesus why he has done this to his parents, Jesus answers: "Why were you seeking (*baqqesh*) me? Did you not know that I must be about my Father's business?" Mary and Joseph did not immediately understand that Jesus was referring to God, but Mary remembered the remark and pondered it frequently. The event foreshadows the fact that Jesus' devotion to the will of God will eventually lead to his leaving Mary and "the people," whom Mary represents, permanently in death, and therefore hints at the "sword" that Simeon had said would pierce the soul of Mary. Jesus cannot, merely because he has been found by *baqqesh*, then turn aside from his painful mission of service to the Father just to please his parents. It is, further, a warning to us all: when we achieve something by *baqqesh*, we must not suppose that what we find must then remain forever as we found it. What we find will, rather, immediately lead us further on.

The Agony in the Garden [*Luke 22:39–46; Mark 14:32–42; Matthew 26:36–46*]

It is the last evening of Jesus' life, and he knows that he is being betrayed to his executioners. After celebrating the Passover supper with his disciples, he retires, as was his custom, to pass the night in Gethsemane, a grove ("garden") on the Mount of Olives. He asks three of his disciples (Peter, James, and John) to "watch" in prayer (i.e. practice *baqqesh*) with him. It becomes a time of intense mental anguish and sorrow for him; he is experiencing the evil of humanity's challenge to God (see pages 37–38). In prayer to the

Father he says "If you are willing, take this cup away from me. Nevertheless, let your will be done, not mine." (These words not only recall the Our Father, but also Jesus' need to be "about my Father's business" as shown in the previous mystery, the Finding.) He receives angelic consolation, but, in his subsequent anguish, his sweat falls from his body in great drops like blood. His disciples, yielding to sleep, fail to support his *baqqesh*. He warns them to pray lest they be caught up in the great trial in which he is engaged. During the night the temple police arrest Jesus, identified to them by the kiss of his disciple Judas.

The Scourging [*Luke 23:13–25; Mark 15:6–15; Matthew 27:15–26; John 19:1*]

On the next day, Governor Pontius Pilate, the Roman administrator, offers to set Jesus free in honor of the Jewish holy day. The crowds cry for Barabbas, an insurrectionist, to be freed instead. Pilate's promise to have Jesus scourged does not satisfy the crowds, and they once again demand Jesus' death. The people get what they seek: Pilate hands Jesus over for crucifixion, preceded by the customary scourging.

The Crowning with Thorns [*Mark 15:16–20; Matthew 27:27–31; John 19:1–3; in Luke 23:25, awareness of the treatment given Jesus and allusion to it but no description of it*]

After scourging Jesus but before leading him to crucifixion, the Roman soldiers mock and torment him (all standard elements of a crucifixion). Blindfolding him, they strike him and demand that he tell, by prophecy, which one struck him. Having heard rumors that Jesus speaks of a kingdom, they clothe him in royal purple robe and put on his head a crown of plaited thorns. They spit on him as they kneel in mock homage. Pilate brings him forth in this condition, but the crowd is not appeased. Jesus is clothed once again in his own robe.

The Way of the Cross [*Luke 23:26–32; Mark 15:21–22; Matthew 27:32–33; John 19:17*]

The technique of crucifixion demands that Jesus carry his own cross. At a certain point along the route to Golgotha, the soldiers, perhaps convinced that Jesus would not otherwise survive to the place of execution, force a passerby, Simon of Cyrene, to take up the cross. Women in the streets weep and wail funeral dirges for Jesus, but he advises them to weep for themselves and for their children (a reference to his foreseeing that Rome would one day treat the whole city as he was being treated). To these scenes Catholics often add details from other traditions of the Church, contemplating, for example, a meeting between Jesus and Mary, and marking the places where Jesus fell while on the way of the cross.

The Death of Jesus [*Luke 23:33–56; Mark 15:22–30; Matthew 27:33–61; John 19:17–42*]

Jesus is nailed to the cross and hoisted up between two others who are being executed as thieves. The crowds mock him while the soldiers divide his garments among themselves, casting lots for the seamless tunic. None of his followers is present to try to comfort him, though at a certain distance some watch. (All are women except one, who was probably too young to be identified as an adult male.) Among these is Mary. In the agony of thirst, Jesus is offered sour wine. He prays and is heard to forgive those who have betrayed him. He consoles one of the thieves, promising they will meet "this day" in the afterlife. He recites at least part of a psalm of lamentation and confidence. After crying out in a loud voice, he dies without having witnessed God's vindication. Soldiers come to break the legs of the crucified ones. This procedure is meant to hasten death and was requested by the Temple leadership to avoid having the execution extend past sundown, when the sabbath would begin. But Jesus is already dead and so his legs are not broken. His side, rather, is pierced with a lance. He is laid in a tomb offered by Joseph of Arimathaea, a secret disciple.

The Resurrection [*Luke 24:1–48; Mark 16; Matthew 28; John 20, 21*]

His search ended now by death, Jesus found that which he sought: the future. In a popular phrase of those days, he was "a man of the world to come." Others said that he was raised from the dead. In this new life the familiar limitations of human existence, which have been our glory and our cross, are transcended. Human nature is not negated but is brought to fulfillments still unimagined.

We do not expect that the risen status of any dead person will be revealed to us prior to the end of the world (the general resurrection) or, at least, prior to our own deaths. Jesus has proved to be an exception, even in death. Compelled now to seek (*baqqesh*) him confusedly in the darkness of sorrow and despair until the third day, his disciples discovered that his tomb, though guarded, was empty. Then, in several experiences of the resurrection, they found Jesus himself.

(Certain women disciples of Jesus found him on the path near the empty tomb. Peter and the twelve had this experience in the "upper room" where they had been hiding; others found him walking on the road to Emmaus. Later a number of disciples found him by the Sea of Galilee.)

Joy and awe went simultaneously through the group of disciples. The news that "Jesus is risen" electrified them, and despair was changed to expectancy. The general resurrection and the end of the world were thought to be imminent.

The Ascension [*Luke 24:49–51; Acts of the Apostles 1:6–11; Mark 16:19–20*]

There was a final event of the sort we describe as experiencing the resurrection; through this event, traditionally called the Ascension, the disciples knew that they would not experience the risen Christ again. They also knew that Jesus would soon give them a mission. Since his mission was ended, theirs, whatever it might be, must begin. It is Luke who describes this final revelation of the resurrection as an ascension, by which he helps us to understand that Jesus is now and for all time glorified and "with the Father." The ascension can just as well be called the exaltation.

At first the Christian community of Jerusalem had been uncertain how it was to function without its absent Lord. But, in the event called the Ascension, it understood by angelic perception (Acts 1:10–11) that, because Jesus had been exalted to the right hand of the Father, God would certainly arrange to "clothe them with power." The disciples understood that their searching (*baqqesh*), which had made it possible for the risen Christ to reveal the resurrection to them, would not allow them to keep him tamely by their side. They returned to Jerusalem to await (*qawweh/baqqesh*) "power from on high." And for the first time we read that Mary was in their midst. She was their closest visible tie to their absent Messiah.

The Descent of the Holy Spirit [*Acts of the Apostles 2:1–41*]

A large group of disciples was assembled in a room in Jerusalem waiting in prayer (*qawweh-baqqesh*) to be clothed in God's power. The power of God had often been described as a fire or even as a wind (wind being, like God, invisible, penetrating, and powerful). Since *wind* and *spirit* are the same word in the biblical languages, it is not surprising that the disciples were awaiting the "power when the Holy Spirit comes down" (Acts 1:8 [NAB]).

At length, when the city of Jerusalem was celebrating the holy day called Pentecost, the gathered disciples, with Mary undoubtedly still in their midst, obtained the results of their *baqqesh*. They underwent a group experience or enlightenment that has determined the course of Church history ever since. They experienced the rushing of the divine wind and the kindling of the divine fire and knew that they had received divine power more than sufficient for their mission, clearly revealed to be to make Jesus known as Messiah and Lord. With their minds and hearts opened as never before, they found wisdom and courage fit for a true Kingdom of God. In the joy of realizing that the messianic age had indeed dawned, the sound of their voices convinced many in Jerusalem that they were drunk. It was a second Nativity, with as many newborn babes as could accept the good news with sincerity and joy. Mary rejoiced, we suppose, to find the infant Church clothed in the same spiritual gifts that she had experienced in her role as mother of the Messiah.

The Assumption of Mary

We humans are very dependent on each other. None of us can expect to overcome all our faults and see ourselves perfected until the day comes when *all* of us can be perfected. Such is our mutual dependency. Thus we do not expect to enjoy the resurrected life before the day when all have arrived in the place of timelessness on the day of the general resurrection.

But Mary had been given the ability to hope for the Kingdom of God with a hope so unselfish and so aligned to God that she made it possible for the Messiah to be entrusted to her. She raised him in the human family. Because of the powers in her, masterpieces of divine initiative and human cooperation, Mary needed not to await the perfection of all the rest of us before obtaining her own fulfillment. She has already found it; she is already fully "assumed" (a word meaning "taken up") into the divine life.

Indeed the Church itself has no powers that Mary did not have first. The Church, for example, begets new Christs by baptism and other influences, but Mary was mother of the *first* Christ. It is fitting, then, that by her assumption, also, Mary should precede the Church.

We do not say that Mary has been raised, for it is not her task to reveal the resurrection. Jesus alone has found that land, has earned that right and ability. But just as death is a kind of falling asleep, so all human beings are destined to awaken. Mary does not show us the resurrection, but the full person (body and soul) that gave Jesus life and education is already awake. She is the Listener. It has often been pointed out that Jesus himself could not really have materiality with God in his future coordinates if he had no one to share it with: material beings are always relational. One defines another. In this mystery, then, we praise Christ for waking Mary in her fullness and thus providing us with the Listener.

The Crowning of Mary as Queen of All Creation

If Mary is fit to be mother of the Messiah, then no one is closer to him in the matter of intercessory prayer (pages 16–17, 21–23, 43–46). Our ancestors, living under monarchical forms of government, expressed the idea that Mary was the peerless intercessor by calling her the Queen. Since Mary has no gifts that were not given to her because of Christ, our ancestors realized that it was Christ who had constituted Mary as Queen of all intercessors. In art, he is shown as giving her the crown. This mystery completes the previous: because Mary is fully awake, our Listener, we merge our prayers in hers.

33. Suggestions for Meditating on the Mysteries

The "Brief Description of the Mysteries" I have just given may well seem confusingly complex and rich in detail. And when the beginner understands that there is much more that remains to be said about each mystery, as we will see in chapter 5, it could very well appear that the rosary is not a school of meditation (concentration of powers) at all, but some sort of theological scrapbook.

I insist, to the contrary, that the Our Father and Hail Mary are basic. The simple presence of God, Christ, and Mary is the unifying force that draws out all our powers. If the beginner will take these two prayers very seriously, using the prompters, then, little by little, the details of the mysteries can be added. As each detail becomes part of the very being of the meditator, it will help to raise him or her to the One. But never must the mysteries be allowed to submerge the meditator's simple prayers.

A. How to Begin

After one's preliminaries (a period of "waiting," then the blessing "In the Name," etc., and possibly the Apostles' Creed, with its own Our Father, three Hail Marys, and Doxology), one says out loud the name of the first joyful mystery: "The Annunciation." The beginner may wish to pause here and review the description of this mystery (pages 91–92), but if this review threatens to become lengthy, it ought to be made before beginning the meditation. Next, one grasps the first isolated bead, which in the case of the first mystery is actually on the preliminary section near the crucifix (see the chart on page xviii), and prays the Our Father as usual. Then one prays ten Hail Marys on the first decade of beads, adding, with one's fingers still on the tenth bead, the Doxology.

B. New Prompters

A few people, particularly those with attentive minds and strong wills, need do no more at this stage. The mere announcement of the first mystery, pronounced before beginning, remains in their minds throughout the whole mystery, influencing the prayer. It is my contention, however, that such people are rare in our culture and, in any case, one may wish to do more, at least as an experiment.

It is always possible to announce the mystery (for example, "The Annunciation") before each Hail Mary. Or one can work the mystery into the first prompter: "I will greet the Lady of the Annunciation, etc."

German Catholics have a tradition of inserting something about the mystery after the name of Jesus. They will say, for example, ". . . and blessed is the fruit of thy womb, Jesus announced." The word *announced* means the same as *annunciation,* but is grammatically easier to insert.

The German method, I find, has much to recommend it. But since I am already recommending the use of prompters, I prefer making the insertion in the second prompter (see page 58):

> "I will praise her son announced: Blessed art thou among women, and blessed is the fruit of thy womb, Jesus."

Easier to remember, though awkward, is the phrase "in the Annunciation," which merely repeats the title of the mystery: "I will praise her son *in the Annunciation*." (The meditator will need to use Appendix Two (page 160), where the prompters described here are presented in full. Column three applies to paragraph C, immediately below, while the columns on page 161 will be used only in chapter 5, where more material on the mysteries is presented.)

C. *Baqqesh* and the Mysteries

All fifteen mysteries involve *baqqesh.* In the Joyful Mysteries, for example, Jesus is sought by Mary (1), Elizabeth (2), the shepherds (3), Simeon and Anna (4), and Mary and Joseph (5). As always, the primary object of *baqqesh* is God; but, in Judeo-Christian-Islamic tradition, God reveals himself best in historical events, such as those that befell Jesus in these mysteries. In the Sorrowful Mysteries, Jesus seeks God's will in each of the five bitter portions of his suffering. In the Glorious Mysteries, God's activity is again sought and found in Jesus: Jesus is found to be risen (1), ascended (2), in the Spirit (3). In the final two mysteries Jesus is found by Mary (4) and by the whole Church (5). Prompters appropriate to these facts can be found in Appendix Two, page 160, column 3.

D. Let the Our Father Be Your Guide

One of the strongest proofs of the "rightness" of rosary meditation is a simple fact that anyone can experience: when you are saying the Our Father, *it* will teach you certain things about whatever mystery you are engaged upon, and it will thus influence the entire mystery if you willingly follow its lead. In the Our Father, for example, we say "Thy Kingdom come." But this will remind us, in the first mystery (Annunciation), that Mary was one who yearned for the Kingdom and hoped for it so purely that God was able to answer her prayer in a decisive way. Or again, "Forgive us our trespasses as we forgive those who trespass against us" reminds us that the *announced* Kingdom for which Mary prays is one of peace, that the Messiah will proclaim peace and forgiveness. There is probably no phrase of the Our Father that may not, at some time or other, take the lead in guiding our meditation on the mystery. A few such reminders for all the mysteries are assembled in Appendix Three.

Similarly, the Hail Mary gives us guidance in each mystery. In the Annunciation, for example, the opening words of the Hail Mary ("Hail Mary, full of grace, the Lord is with thee") are the very words addressed to Mary by the angel in the original annunciation. The words of the prayer, if prayed slowly and thoughtfully, cannot help but prompt us to be aware of the Annunciation. In the Visitation, it is the central words of the Hail Mary ("Blessed art thou among women, and blessed is the fruit of thy womb") that suggest the mystery itself, since it was during the Visitation that Elizabeth said these words to Mary. In the Nativity, it may well be the word *theotokos* ("Mother of God") that leaps out at us.

These associations will eventually *work backward* to improve the quality of the Our Fathers, which begin each mystery. I will say "Thy Kingdom come," for example, with all the power that comes of knowing what the Kingdom meant to Mary, to Elizabeth, to the shepherds, to Simeon, and to the young Church of Pentecost. The mere name of the mystery will bring the proper attitude to bear on the neighboring Our Father.

34. Further Suggestions

A. As the number of Hail Marys begins to grow, resist the temptation to take them less seriously. Try to think, at the beginning of each Hail Mary (before saying the prompter "I must address Mary" and moving your fingers on the beads) that you are approaching her *anew*. (Sometimes I pretend that twenty years have gone by since my last Hail Mary! This is no mere trick: people like Mary have stepped out of the stream of time and will meet us at any time for which we reach.)

B. Be content, for at least a few days, with the first two or three Joyful Mysteries.[30]

---

[30] It is not recommended, in any case, that the beginner employ mysteries other than the fifteen that have become traditional. While additional myster-

C. Recall (page 58) that the prompters are eventually to be *intended only*, not spoken.

D. Keep faithful to your journal; if some new variation for the second prompter of the Hail Mary should occur to you, write it down, use it, and record your experience with it.

E. Try to insure that your awareness of the Father's presence *lasts* through all ten Hail Mary's. This is important, for meditation is designed to be a *unitive* approach to reality. Everything we do in meditation should increasingly focus on the single point, which is God.

Of paramount importance, here, is the third section of the Hail Mary. When correctly meditated upon, it directs our whole energy toward the Father (see pages 44–46).

There are additional helps to ensuring continued awareness of the Father: thinking of yourself as firstborn heir to the father's "business" (pages 68–69) should help. Letting the "Our Father be your guide" (pages 103–4, 162–68), should be another aid. It is well to ask God specifically, before you announce the name of each mystery, to help you penetrate that mystery. Recall, too, that at the end of the mystery you are going to give God a Doxology. Ask Mary to help you with your Doxology and try to make the Our Father and Doxology, at opposite ends of the mystery, "touch." The expression "Mother of God" can strengthen your awareness of the Father ten times in each mystery.

35. Biblical Studies and the Mysteries

The Bible is not the *immediate* source of rosary meditation: one does not simply go from the New Testament to the rosary. Yet because the mysteries are firmly grounded in the Bible and because of the great advances that have been made in modern biblical studies, the subject requires more comment here.

---

ies were at one time popular and are still being proposed, the characteristic and fundamental mysteries of the rosary are those of Luke.

One of the leading insights of modern biblical studies concerns the roles of the four evangelists, Matthew, Mark, Luke, and John (to use the names assigned to them by tradition). The four Gospels, we now know, do not give us the life and teachings of Jesus only, but also the benefit of the experiences of each of the four gospel writers and of the churches with which they were associated in the decades following the death of Jesus. Luke, in his Gospel and his Acts of the Apostles (a sort of sequel to the Gospel), has given us most of the rosary mysteries; all studies that clarify his intentions in writing these two books have the potential of shedding light on the mysteries.[31]

Many of Luke's insights are incorporated in this book, especially in the two units on the mysteries (chapters 4 and 5). Other Lucan themes, such as those closely connected to problems of his day, receive less treatment here.

Wilfrid Harrington's excellent book *The Rosary: A Gospel Prayer* (see page xiiin.) addresses this point expressly. Harrington treats all fifteen mysteries, though he goes beyond Luke to provide material from the other three evangelists.

While my book gives great emphasis to Luke, the Sorrowful Mysteries require a slightly different treatment. It is clear that narratives of the suffering and death of Christ were widely circulated among Christians even before our present Gospels were written. Luke is very respectful of the earlier shape of these narratives and inserts his own concerns much less frequently here than in those mysteries for which he had exclusive sources. Additionally, there can be no doubt that Christians had meditated on the sufferings and death of Jesus well before Luke wrote his Gospel. Thus all four Gospels contribute to my treatment of the Sorrowful Mysteries.

I have referred above (pages 91, 92) to the fact that the Gospel text is too rich in details to serve as the immediate basis for rosary meditation. The Gospels are narratives and teach their lessons

---

[31] See "Further Readings" for Leonard Doohan's *Luke: The Perennial Spirituality*.

primarily through narrative style. Without lessening the importance of this warning, it remains true that Harrington succeeds admirably in highlighting the New Testament teachings on Christ, teachings that appear in the New Testament's treatment of each mystery. While my book also reflects the New Testament teaching on Christ, many readers will want to verify this for themselves with the help of a book such as Harrington's.

Wilfrid Harrington's book serves well, also, as an introduction to the complexity of modern biblical studies: he exposes this complexity while finding pathways through it. Although I do not necessarily recommend that his book be read at this stage of our journey through rosary meditation, it is a book that most rosary meditators not already schooled in modern biblical studies will want to read eventually.[32]

I have, perhaps, explained sufficiently (page 92n.) why it is that I accept events in Luke's mysteries at face value as ideal for meditation, without exploring how the events depicted may have been understood during the several decades between the death of Christ and the writing of Luke. This willingness to accept events as narrated is, however, far from fundamentalism. I hold, on the contrary, that many of the older passages in the Bible can, with due cautions, be taken as foreshadowings of later events in biblical history, whereas later texts may occasionally be taken as allegories of earlier events. Sometimes the authors of the Bible interpret earlier parts of the Bible in this way, and I assume that the method can be valid even in cases when the Bible does not pause to confirm my conjectures. I assume further that biblical narratives of events may also symbolize the inner life of human spirituality. There is a sense, too, in which ordinary Jewish and Christian experience ("tradition") can sometimes be used as a guide to interpretation. Finally, modern biblical studies have taught us to read biblical passages in the light of the type of literature, written or oral, that each passage originally was.

---

32 See also Pheme Perkins, *Reading the New Testament*, 2d Edition (Mahwah, N.J.: Paulist Press, 1988).

The variety of these and other ways of interpretation can cause readers to think that plain biblical facts are being denied in a book such as this one. It should be remembered, however, that supernatural events, or events "from the future," are more wonderful—not less wonderful—than the plain sense of Scripture might lead us to believe. Words have their limits, and even a biblical description of the resurrection, for example, cannot do justice to the event.

5

The Mysteries in Greater Depth

Rosary meditation could develop for a lifetime simply on the basis of the material presented in the first four chapters. To rush to the present section, chapter 5, as though mere writings such as this book were the real sources of progress in the rosary, would be to forget the most important point: that God is the ultimate orchestrator of our spiritual lives. A beginner may well pause many weeks before peeping into this section. The rosary should have become a positive joy before one leaves chapter 4. Our ability to lift up our hearts and minds should have become very noticeably improved. Most of all, some of the events of our daily lives should begin to influence, and be influenced by, the rosary. Our journals should give testimony to that influence.

(By now the meditator may have found his or her rosary moving occasionally along paths not discussed in this book. Sometimes this may be related to the personalized language of events that God speaks to each of us. Others may have unique spiritual gifts or needs. The journal is now doubly important, for it is becoming an authentic new book on the rosary.)

36. The Annunciation in Greater Depth

[*Luke 1:26–38*]

[For prompters for this series, see Appendix Two, page 161, column one. See also pages 87–90, which treat the miraculous element in the Annunciation].

In the Bible, God's people are repeatedly imprisoned either spiritually (by their own sins) or physically (by enemies). God, in his turn, repeatedly pays his people's ransom or "redeems" them (literally "buys them back"). The result is liberation.

The biblical story of the Annunciation does not mention that one of Jesus' missions will be to free God's people for the last time by giving the ultimate price of their redemption and liberation. Nor did Mary then know what she would later know, that the death of her son would be counted as the people's last ransom. But it is common New Testament teaching that Jesus was a liberator or savior and that his whole life and death were redemptive.

Christians usually think of Jesus as redeeming us from the prisons we build through our own mistakes. From this point of view, many question how it is that rosary meditation can assign such high praise to the young woman who happened to give birth to the redeemer. At the time of the Annunciation, it is argued, no one had as yet been redeemed, not even Mary.

This problem, which looms large for many, would seem to be an unnecessary obstacle. There had been, after all, many good people before Mary. How were *they* able to be so pleasing to God if they were not yet redeemed from their sins? Would it not be more helpful to recall that God played a part in the nurturing of all these good human acts from the beginning of time? And did not God nurture these acts *in anticipation* of the fact that he would approve one human life, that of Jesus, as sufficient to end all talk of further ransoms?

There is no time in God: with him a redemptive event can work backwards in time as well as forwards. This way of looking at things allows us to suppose that Mary, in the Annunciation, is already a redeemed person. Because her life would focus all the *baqqesh* of previous centuries, she needed to be a lens of perfect clarity. She needed to feel the fruits of full rescue, full redemption, during her entire development as a person. (This is what Catholics call Mary's Immaculate Conception. The term is often mistaken as pertaining to the virginal conception of Jesus.)

While Luke was not grappling with the redemption problem when he penned his Annunciation narrative, he does portray Mary as one who has found favor with God, one upon whom the Holy Spirit is descending for the purpose of giving the world a new Son of God. Certainly the rosary is not the place for exercises in theology: it is sufficient here to note the unique place in history that the Annunciation assigns to Mary.

The Annunciation, if it was anything, was a communication. Modern philosophers and psychologists have put much thought on the question of what communication really is. Many of the valuable insights gained have filtered down to diplomats, corporate managers, family counselors, and, above, all, advertisers. One of the principal new insights is that a communication is not a communication unless it renders the recipient capable of receiving the message offered *with all its consequences*. Thus, we may be sure that Mary was prepared, in advance, for her all-important function in the life of the new Adam. And perhaps Mary's preparation would have revealed itself best in unrivaled hope.

Mary had "resurrection-hope," already in the Annunciation.

I have said that there is no limit to God's willingness to give us good things, though he is restricted, in a sense, by our attitudes. If humanity at large had begun to hope in the pure sense, the world would have been changed in the twinkling of an eye, and the Kingdom of God would have fully arrived. But if even one human being hoped with sufficient unselfishness, confidence, and intensity, God could at least *begin* the final era of the world as we know it. Can there be any doubt, in view of who her son was, that Mary was that one?

The hope that Mary brought to the Annunciation can well be called "resurrection-hope." Perhaps Mary did not think much about the word *resurrection*. Most of the Jews who believed in resurrection saw it as an act of God, bursting into our world with his final Kingdom and raising innocent victims of persecution so that they might be vindicated. Mary's circle did not worry a great deal about the exact nature of resurrected life but hoped earnestly for God's Kingdom to be realized quickly among his people.

If Mary did not think much about resurrection, we can be quite sure that her ideas on the subject did not range forward to the concept we now have: that the resurrection is the fulfillment of all human potential. But though Mary did not think about this definition, her hope-filled intuition of God's goodness must have been rich enough to include it in principle. If anyone had explained the concept of the "fulfilling of all human potential," she would certainly have acknowledged that God would give us that, if we would let him. Doubtless, too, she had many individual hopes that, when added together, would presume something like the resurrection. Thus, we say that Mary had resurrection-hope even if she expended little thought on the matter.

Similarly, we say that the human existence of Jesus is uniquely rooted in divine uncreated existence, for that is part of what we mean by calling Jesus "the Son of God." Mary did not speculate about types of existence, the created and the uncreated, yet her hope was strong enough to allow God to embrace this world so fully as to offer his divine existence as the point upon which would rest the humanity of her child.

Although Mary had resurrection-hope, God could not reveal the resurrection in the flesh of the infant Jesus. But, as we have seen by looking at miracles, Mary did give birth to the child who was already the resurrection-man, the man of the future. Even the manner of Jesus' conception could be reminiscent of the powers of the resurrection. When a person has hope pure enough to allow the dawning of the Age of the Messiah, God is enabled to reveal many new things that are brought forward from the future state of resurrection.

I have said (page 91) that the Annunciation is the most important of the mysteries, at least in the sense that it contains the assumptions upon which all our meditation rests. The rule that Mary had to be prepared in advance, by a purification that resulted in unselfish hope, is the same rule that governs *all* prayer and meditation: God is already helping to purify our hopes that he may fulfill them. All prayer is pregnancy.

It is also clear that Luke regarded Mary as a prophet. Not only is she given a message by an angel, but she, like the prophets of the Old Testament, designates herself as servant of the Lord and obedient to the word of God ("Behold the servant of the Lord; be it done to me in accord with your word" [Luke 1:38]).[33]

Wherever Mary goes, during her pregnancy and during the childhood of Jesus, her "burden" is joyously received, according to Luke's depictions of the mysteries. Mary does not even have to speak her prophetic message: it is sufficient that she store up everything in her heart (Luke 2:19, 51). As Jesus once says elsewhere when Mary is mentioned (Luke 11:28 [NAB]), "Blest are they who hear the word of God and keep it."[34] Mary's speech has become what the speech of many prophets of the Old Testament became—what we hope our own speech will someday be—a language of events like God's.

Luke, of course, did not give us this mystery so that he could indulge a private Marian devotion; rather, the mystery is meant for us. We are meant to wish that we too could be caught up in a hope like Mary's and of course, says Luke, we can.

[Review also Appendix Three, page 162, under "Annunciation."]

37. The Visitation in Greater Depth

[*Luke 1:39–56*]

If the Annunciation is the mystery of purified hope, we can say that the Visitation is the mystery of faith (trust). In the Annunciation, Mary's hope, displayed in all its grandeur, makes possible the announcement of the good news concerning the Messiah. In the Visitation we see Mary *trusting* in the revelation that had been

---

[33] Richard J. Sklba, "Mary and the *Anawim*," in *Mary, Woman of Nazareth: Biblical and Theological Perspecitves*, ed. Doris Donnelly (New York: Paulist Press, 1989), page 123.

[34] Donald Senior, "A Gospel Portrait of Mary," in *Mary: Woman of Nazareth* (op. cit.), page 95.

made to her. The fact that Elizabeth uses words normally reserved for congratulating a woman *after* childbirth ("Blessed art thou among women") shows that both women have full confidence in God's promise respecting the child.

In our own lives we sometimes find ourselves not believing good news when it is announced to us. We distrust it, thinking it is too good, it will turn bad, it will ask too much of us. These unworthy feelings gave Mary no pause. She went immediately, "with haste," to the hill country of Judah in which Elizabeth lived.

Elizabeth, too, showed faith. Whether she knew of Mary's having conceived the Messiah by previous angelic perception, or only knew it as Mary approached her (this is the sort of question that did not interest the gospel writers), she knew it and accepted it in faith. She believed, and praised Mary for having believed. "Blest is she who trusted that the Lord's words to her would be fulfilled" (Luke 1:45 [NAB]).

In the theology of the Bible, God often makes visitations, especially to his people Israel. The descriptions of such visits are modeled after those of the contemporary imperial authorities: the emperor or his representative visits, makes an official inquiry, and punishes or rewards the province or city he is visiting. Thus the early Israelite prophets, who were shocked by the injustices in Israelite life, often warned about the day of God's visitation. More recently voices had rejoiced in the coming visitation, since it would bring a new Israel, a "buying back" (redemption) of imprisoned Israel, and a resurrection of the just. In the words of the Canticle of Zachary (Elizabeth's husband), recorded by Luke after the fact:

Blessed be the Lord, the God of Israel,
  for he has made a visitation and redeemed his people,
Raising up a horn of salvation
  in the House of David, his servant.

[*Luke 1:68–69: Zachary's Canticle.*]
[*author's translation*]

For us rosary meditators, then, the Visitation is not just Mary's visitation of Elizabeth, but it is *God's* visitation of Elizabeth. Elizabeth discerns the divine grace in the coming of Mary and her unborn child.

There is a depth of mystery about this Visitation. The emperor (God) is invisible; his viceroy (Jesus) is an infant hidden in the womb. Like most mysteries suitable for *baqqesh,* the scene is all potential, pointing to the future. There is no severity here, no adverse judgment against us who are visited, unless we have come to the sorry pass of being unjust to faith-filled women and babes. We dare to express our own hopes to our royal visitors and their noble friends. We trust them.

Since God's visit to Elizabeth is only carried out through the cooperation of Mary, we have here a fine picture of Mary as our Sponsor (see again number 25). Mary, in effect, presents Elizabeth to the God who visits her. Elizabeth, who recognizes Mary's favored relationship both to God and to his Messiah, doubtless rejoices to have obtained their visitation through her relationship with Mary, her informal sponsor.

It would have been natural, too, if Elizabeth asked Mary to pray for her. Elizabeth thus stands at the head of a long line of those who make Mary their Sponsor, Listener, and Intercessor. Elizabeth even recognizes Mary's presence as a precious blessing upon herself and her household, which is one reason why she uses the word "blessed" of Mary and her son: in ancient Judaic thought, persons *blessed* by God are themselves *blessings* for others.

In the Annunciation, Mary is "evangelized," and that by a revelation from God through an angel. In the Visitation, the good news takes its first step into the messianic community. Elizabeth, a woman of hopes similar to Mary's, is evangelized. And it was not what Mary said, but her merely having brought her unborn child to Elizabeth, that constituted the evangelization.

In this mystery, we take the place of Elizabeth and receive a Visitation of God. We welcome the new Adam in faith, just as, in the Annunciation, we strove to purify our hope for him. In a sense, all the mysteries of the rosary are God's visitations, just as they are all the result of our seeking.

[Review also Appendix Three, page 162, under "Visitation."]

38. The Nativity in Greater Depth

[*Luke 2:1–20*]

As the Annunciation stirs our hopes, and the Visitation encourages our faith (trust), so the Nativity taps our powers of love.

It is difficult to love that which is not yet seen, and in this mystery Jesus first appears. But there is more: are we being merely sentimental to suggest that this mystery draws from us some of the feeling we have for all infants and children, particularly our own?

The charge of sentimentality might have some basis, for many who will not follow the adult Jesus in his more challenging sayings profess to love the babe of Christmas. But the instinct to love the infant cannot be dismissed with such cynicism. A child, lacking the developed gifts, reveals humanity as such. There is a beauty about humanity, a beauty that calls forth love.

Here, again, the presence of Mary is extremely important. No one will doubt the validity of the love given a child by its own parents, and Mary's love for Jesus strikes resonant vibrations within ourselves. The dependency of a child on its parents' love is most graphically seen in infancy. A child cannot even be realistically represented in art without its parents, as we can learn most easily from Christmas cards: the child is always with Mary and Joseph.

It is said that the first crèche, or Nativity scene, was constructed by that furnace of divine love, Francis of Assisi, who has never been accused of mere sentimentality. Probably, too, none of the mysteries has been painted so often as this. Any love we extend to Jesus in this mystery will have to mature through the subsequent mysteries, as Mary's own love for him matured, but it is safely rooted in the Nativity.

All the joyful mysteries are quiet scenes, as though they were designed as so many cubicles where one might meditate. No one needs to be reminded of the silence of Christmas eve, with its shepherds' fields, its starry sky, and its soft-spoken beasts. As a newborn, the child is all potential and makes us think of the grand sweep of life. We instinctively banish pettiness and think kindly of others. Everything is perfect for the Our Father or the Hail Mary.

Many people admire Jesus in a noncommittal way; others see him as a person they can use in one way or another. Mary teaches us to give him unfeigned love. It distresses some to think of attempting to love someone long dead, however admirable. But any system of meditation that did *not* touch the human heart could never take us to the depth of being.

The evangelization that began with Mary (Annunciation) and spread to an intimate branch of the messianic community (Visitation to Elizabeth), here, in the Nativity, embraces strangers. But they are not just any strangers. They are shepherds, the poorest of Israel's poor. If God thus favors those who are often (unfairly) thought to be of the lowest attainments, he favors human nature as such, stripped of pretensions. Not for nothing does the angelic revelation (Luke 2:10) speak of joy "for the whole people," not limited to any particular class.

Luke often elevates the poor as a way of elevating humanity as such. But it is more than Luke's literary genius that remembers that Jesus had to be laid in a manger, a sign of the utter helplessness of his parents to provide anything better: the poverty of the Christ child is surely a memory treasured by Mary. It could not have been invented.

In antiquity, the emergence of a great leader from poverty was often taken as a confirmation of God's special predilection for that leader. Moses had been born of a helpless Hebrew family and had to be laid in a basket and trusted to the Nile: his people had no other way of saving his life from the Egyptians. The founders of Akkad and Rome had similar experiences. King David was the least likely of the sons of Jesse but was taken from the very shepherds' fields of Bethlehem to become King of Israel. Against this background we can understand why memories of Jesus' poverty were preserved. But when Luke heard of them, he used them to show that the good news was meant for all, beginning with the poor.

In meditating on the Nativity we may, if we choose, think of the coming of the Magi, as depicted in Matthew 2. But the Magi narrative is Matthew's way of describing for us the evangelization of foreign nations, something that Luke reserves for the next mystery. It may be preferable to follow Luke's scheme, since he is the original author of the Joyful Mysteries.

The angel of the Nativity is reported as saying, "Glory to God in the high heavens; peace on earth, good will toward men." These words are a close echo of the Our Father's "Thy [good] will be done, on earth as it is in heaven."

[Review also Appendix Three, page 163, under "Nativity."]

39. The Presentation in Greater Depth

[*Luke 2:22–40*]

The Holy Family go to the temple for the Presentation of Jesus and for what is called the Purification of Mary, though it would be more accurate to call it the Refreshment of Mary.

Jewish law held that childbirth, though one of the most blessed of events, disqualified a mother, temporarily, from participating in Jewish ritual. There were many such disqualifications in Jewish law, but a visit to the temple would usually remove any of them. The word "purification" comes from the fact that many Jewish "disqualifiers" were related to contact with unwholesome things, such as tainted meats, infections, and the like, but there was no implication that *all* such disqualifiers were somehow dirty or repulsive.

In the case of childbirth, though a mother has given birth to new life, she herself has had a brush with death. The rituals of the God of Israel always attempt to disassociate him from the rites of the underworld, whose god was widely worshipped among Israel's neighbors. A new mother, like all survivors in Israel, must go back to the house of God to be recertified for ritual. And by going to the temple she implicitly acknowledges that God is the giver of life.

The redemption of the firstborn by the offering of lambs or doves seems originally to have been part of Israel's campaign against child sacrifice, a horror not infrequently practiced in the region. The doves were a substitute for the death of the child. But this practice, like the ritual for the mother, had come to make the point that all life is from God.

We notice that the Holy Family are represented as being very faithful to the Jewish law and the ordinary forms of devotion. It would not have occurred to them to think that they or their child might be "above the Law." Yet the meditator may well notice the ironies: she whose hopes were an open invitation to the Spirit of God and the new Adam, accepted the fact that she could be prohibited from ritual until she had new contact with God in the temple. She who was herself a shrine in which God had acted, went willingly to the more public shrine to acknowledge her creaturely dependence on God. And he who is believed to have redeemed others for God was redeemed *from* God (so that he could grow up at home) by the price of two doves.

The Presentation is the only mystery drawn by Luke that places us at a liturgy. We may wonder about this, as liturgies, at least in this divided age, are often unconducive to prayer. Jesus, in fact, complained about the temple being no longer a house of prayer (Mark 11:15–19). Sometimes, however, we are privileged to participate in a liturgy in which there are participants who move, unself-consciously, in the presence of God. Such were Simeon and Anna, meditators like us, who had long awaited (*qawweh/baqqesh*) the "expectation of Israel." Such, of course, were Mary and Joseph.

If hope, faith, and love are recalled by the first three mysteries, the Presentation speaks of the *gratitude* that the aged Simeon felt merely to have lived long enough to see the Messiah. Thankfulness, among all human attitudes, is particularly suited to open us to the real, to the incredible fact of our own existence. Both Simeon and Anna react as did Elizabeth: with gratitude for this visit paid them by a child in arms.

The Presentation reminds us that love, which we felt in the Nativity, must be that high sort of love that lets the beloved be free to follow his or her own mission from God. God accepts the two doves, but he makes it clear, through the voice of Simeon, that more will be exacted of Jesus and of his mother. Jesus will be the light of the nations but also a sign that will be contradicted, while Mary will feel a sword piercing her soul. That we must set the beloved free is the lesson of parenthood itself, here beginning to make additional demands on Mary, demands that will only increase through the remaining mysteries.

By now the reader will have noticed one of the glories of the rosary: it attaches us to persons, but these persons are presented in situations that we all must face. (Recall the "human" captions for the mysteries in number 30.) We all, for example, can be parents or at least have analogous experiences. To be adept in meditation, we need to live justly, wisely, and lovingly in each stage of life. Meditation is not the main factor that *makes* us good, but neither is meditation something that can be accomplished readily by a person who does not at least *strive* to be good.

The testimony of Simeon and Anna amazes Mary and Joseph. It is not that they are hearing for the first time that the Kingdom will be brought by Jesus. But the continually widening circle of those who acknowledge the child touches their sense of wonder. Evangelization has gone from Mary to the messianic community (Elizabeth), to all Israel (the shepherds), and now extends to a prophet at the national temple who speaks of a "light of the nations."

In the Presentation we think of "Hallowed be thy Name," for the temple was built precisely to be the place where God's Name is hallowed. By being brought there, Jesus, in fact, is bringing the Name into the holy house, giving the house a new consecration.

[Review also Appendix Three, p. 163, under "Presentation."]

40. The Finding in the Temple in Greater Depth

[*Luke 2:41–52*]

At the age of twelve, Jesus is *bar mitzvah* ("Son of the Law"), and he takes upon himself the obligations of an Israelite. But he is "Son of the Law" in a new sense as well. We may understand "Law" here not merely as the prescriptions of the Mosaic code but also as the Mind and Good Will of God in a more intense form. The Kingdom is coming and will be brought about not by legislation, even of divine origin, but by divine example. And, as in the previous mystery, we think of "Hallowed be thy Name." Once again the scene is the Temple, the place that was built for the Name. Jesus is not only *bar mitzvah,* he is *bar shem* ("Son of the Name").

The missing Jesus is found on the third day. Just as the Church "lost" Jesus until the third day, so, here, as always, Mary and Joseph *precede* the Church. The mystery tells us, then, what it is like to be a person for whom Jesus is missing, a person with no Easter (we have all been that person at some time or other). It teaches us to long and to search.

We praise Jesus, in this mystery, precisely for being "about his Father's business," a restatement of his frequent theme "Thy will be done." Here we have the central Christian teaching: God loves us, so we ought to trust him, but trusting him means attempting to know and do his will. It is well to remember that, as in the other mysteries where Jesus seems to be missing (Ascension, Spirit-sending, Assumption, Crowning), Jesus is the active presence, though he is "about his Father's business."

Here are prefigured all those nights when Jesus, as we read, went up a hill or to a deserted place to commune with the Father, and all those days when he went about following the Father's instructions. Like a typical firstborn in the Near East, Jesus sees his role as that of the Son who is manager of his Father's estate (see page 68). He serves his Father faithfully and will one day inherit. Meanwhile, the whole estate is for his use, and he daily puts trust in the provident care of his Father. No one can be excluded from his love, since the Father blesses all. As we meditate on this mystery, we long for the day when Mary will find us, too, fully occupied doing "the Father's business."

Mary's hope was sufficient to allow the coming of the Son of God, but that does not mean she understood at once all that is implied in such sonship. It will be revealed to her step by step. The sword that pierces her soul will increasingly appear, but so will the joy of finding Jesus again and bringing him home.

The learned men of the temple are astounded by Jesus' intelligence and his answers. As the Presentation speaks to us of gratitude, so the Finding speaks to us of the wonder evoked by Jesus, though we must also admire his devotion to the Father and the joy of his parents upon finding him again.

[Review also Appendix Three, page 164, under "The Finding in the Temple."]

41. The Joy in the Joyful Mysteries

Enough has been said, I hope, to clarify the prompters that are listed under the Joyful Mysteries in Appendix Two, page 161, column one. But a further word must be said about column two.

Scholars have long recognized that joy is a particular theme of Luke's. The Joyful Mysteries, then, are well named, for they come to us from Luke. And Mary was a joyful person: she knew, before Jesus said it, that "it is more blessed to give than to receive."

Good people (and we are all good sometimes!) have an instinct for rejoicing in the good of others. The heart that loves God also rejoices to see him loved, praised, honored, and served, no matter by whom. Mary, we may be sure, hoped for the Kingdom of God not only for humanity's benefit, but in order that God might be better pleased by his human family. Although God is never unhappy, the devout soul hopes that its own love for God may strike a chord of joy in the heart of God.

Mary understood, of course (Annunciation, Luke 1:26–38), that the child to be born would be someone in whom God would rejoice, and it surely gave Mary joy to think that she would be allowed to play a part in giving God that joy. Every parent can say as much, for every child born can bring God joy. But not every child brings, like Mary's child, the Kingdom of God in its fullness. As a prompter for the Annunciation (see column two, page 161), one may well say "I will praise her son, joy of Mary, joy of the Father."

In the Visitation (Luke 1:39–56), Mary rejoices to find that her son is already the joy of Elizabeth, who represents the community of those in Israel who hope for the messianic Kingdom. Jesus is "Joy of Elizabeth."

Luke's story of the Nativity (Luke 2:1–20) contains the words of the angel, "I bring you news of great joy, a joy to be shared by all the people." The shepherds, as we have said, themselves represent "all the people," since they have no wealth or privilege except their very humanity.

In the Presentation (Luke 2:22–40), a joyful Simeon gazes out over the whole world and describes Jesus as "light of the nations." He is, then, "joy of all nations."

Mary and Joseph experience the great joy of finding the missing Jesus (Luke 2:41–52). But he is also, as in the first Joyful Mystery, the joy of the Father, whose business he so faithfully carries on.

42. The Sorrowful Mysteries in Greater Depth

[*Luke 22:39–23:56; Mark 14:32–15:47; Matthew 26:36–27:61; John 18:1–19:42*]

The Sorrowful Mysteries are all segments of a single great mystery, the passion (Latin: *passio,* "suffering") and death of the Lord. Thus we will treat them as a group.

Among the phrases of the Our Father, "Thy will be done" is undoubtedly the most significant for the Sorrowful Mysteries. This idea is clearly singled out in the first Sorrowful Mystery ("Not my will, but thine be done," Luke 22:42), and in the remaining four mysteries Jesus abides by "thy [God's] will," whatever the cost. (It should not be thought, however, that God ever directly wills suffering and death, even in the case of Jesus. Rather, God wills love, witness, service, and sacrifice, things that sometimes make death the only alternative.)

The praise of Jesus takes on a new element in the Sorrowful Mysteries. We still praise Jesus because of the way he conducted himself in the Agony, the Scourging, and the rest. But now, in a sense, we also praise him *notwithstanding these events.* The sufferings of Jesus were regarded by his enemies and friends as a terrible disgrace. Many left him because of them. In praising Jesus to Mary, we wish to state that we remain with Jesus, despite, or notwithstanding, the humiliation he suffered. We profess ourselves not to be scandalized by his manner of execution.

Needless to say, Mary no longer needs to be consoled over the sufferings of her son. She is in bliss. But we may place ourselves in her former situation and offer our loyalty. Meditation abolishes time: what we say now in prayer can really affect Mary and Jesus in their former situation.

It is easy for us, now, to say that we are not scandalized by Jesus. We were not there to see what happened. But we may take the Sorrowful Mysteries to include all the humiliations that the name and honor of Jesus Christ still suffer. He is still held in contempt by many, and we still are asked not to desert him by living unworthily of him.

Additionally, we ought to keep in mind the continual suffering of human beings everywhere, whom Jesus designated as his brothers and sisters, all invited or actual members of his mystical body. Prompters have been devised that reflect these sufferings (see Appendix Two, page 161, column three):

I will praise her Son, sorrowing with all people.
I will praise her Son, scourged with the downtrodden.
I will praise her Son, mocked with the weak.
I will praise her Son, carrying the burdens of the enslaved.
I will praise her Son, innocently dying with the innocent.

Mary was not present at the Agony, the Scourging, or the Crowning with Thorns. The New Testament does not record that she met Jesus on the Way of the Cross (though she might well have done so, as the traditions of the Stations of the Cross tell us). Matthew, Mark, and Luke do not list Mary as being with the other women who witnessed Jesus' death, and this has led many commentators to suppose that John's description of Mary's presence near the cross (John 19:26–27) was originally only a dramatization of Mary's spiritual presence, or of the Church's presence. Whatever the truth or falsity of this last idea, it is clear that it is best not to try to imagine Mary participating directly in the events behind the Sorrowful Mysteries. But she learned of them soon after, had doubtless anticipated them, and is very well aware of them now!

What we will say to Mary, the mother, about the horrible suffering and death of her Son is, of course, very personal to each of us. It is well to remember, however, that what Mary most wishes to hear is praise of Jesus.

It may sometimes be helpful to kneel and look upon the rosary's crucifix during the fifth sorrowful mystery. During all the Sorrowful Mysteries, for that matter, we mingle our own sufferings with those of Jesus. We also know that we too have persecuted the innocent, so we approach Mary the more fervently requesting that she "pray for us sinners now and at the hour of our death."

[Review also Appendix Three, pages 164–66, under the various sorrowful mysteries.]

43. The Sorrowful Mysteries as a Passover

[See Appendix Two, page 162, column two]

From earliest times, Christians compared the suffering, death, and resurrection of Jesus with the Passover and Exodus of the Hebrews as described in the Book of Exodus in the Bible. Additionally, Jesus was compared with Moses or even with the paschal lamb of the Passover story. Our Sorrowful Mysteries contain many instances of this Passover symbolism. Because this symbolism, now part of our culture for more than three thousand years, can greatly arouse the powers of meditation within us, the subject seems to deserve separate treatment here.

A. The Agony in the Garden [*Luke 22:39–46; Mark 14:32–34; Matthew 26:36–46*]

According to the Book of Exodus, the Hebrews had been enslaved in Egypt for nearly four hundred years at the time of Moses' birth. Although Moses was a Hebrew, he was brought up as an Egyptian prince. But Moses grieved deeply for the sufferings of his fellow Hebrews, and he took it upon himself to do something. His initial attempts were discovered by the Egyptians, and he had to flee the country. He settled near Mt. Sinai, becoming a shepherd. One day, still sorrowing for his people, he had an experience of God (the burning bush) and was assured that God had heard the cries of the people. God, moreover, commissioned Moses to return to Egypt and lead the people forth. Moses felt unequal to the task but, upon being made aware that God would not change his mind, he accepted the will of God.

It is helpful to try to see Jesus' passion as similar, though exceeding, that of Moses. Jesus, like Moses, grieved over the sorrows of the people, though his compassion included the sorrows of all humanity. (Had Jesus been present in ancient Egypt, he would have sorrowed for the Egyptians as well as for the Israelites.) Jesus had to avoid Jerusalem at times, for much the same reasons as Moses had to flee Egypt: the authorities had decided to kill him. Jesus was alone on the Mount of Olives much as Moses was alone on Mt. Sinai. On the Mount of Olives, Jesus felt all the sorrows of the people, to the extent that he approached death itself. Like Moses, he had an experience of God giving him a fearful commission that (as we know from other biblical passages) would free the people. And Jesus, again like Moses, struggled over the terrors of the task but accepted it to be the will of God that he should not flee his persecutors but remain to give his testimony to Jerusalem. (Exodus 1–4)

B. The Scourging at the Pillar [*Luke 23:13–25; Mark 15:6–15; Matthew 27:15–26; John 19:1*]

According to the story of Exodus, ten dreadful calamities fell upon the Egyptians because, on Moses' return to Egypt, they still refused to liberate the Israelites. These calamities are traditionally called the ten plagues. (The word *plague* [Latin: *plaga*] originally meant simply the blow of a rod striking someone. Disasters came to be called "plagues" in the sense of blows.) Just as Jesus entered fully into our sorrows in the Agony in the Garden, so in the Scourging he experienced great pain, another dreaded feature of our world, as he felt the blows (plagues) of the whip.

God does not enjoy seeing people suffer. Yet it is one of the glories of our world that we can remain committed to love and justice despite the difficulties of living in a world of fragile matter. Things can go wrong here, painfully wrong. Force breaks us, water drowns us, fire burns us, disease attacks us. Unless we wish to give up the challenge of the human condition and live as angels, we must expect such calamities. But however bravely we live in this world, the blows may still hurt dreadfully. By accepting the scourging, Jesus is, again, accepting the human condition itself.

But let us note the difference! In the original Exodus, the Egyptians were not freed from their "plagues." Like most of us, the Egyptians intensified the plagues through their own folly. It was not their hour of salvation. But Jesus, demonstrating the principle "Love your enemies," takes the plagues upon himself, even though he is the deliverer, not the persecutor. (Exodus 5–11)

C. The Crowning with Thorns [*Mark 15:16–20; Matthew 27:27–31; John 19:1–13; Luke 23:25*]

On the night of the first Passover, which was also the night of their escape, the Hebrews ate the Passover meal, for which a lamb was sacrificed. The blood of the lamb was sprinkled on the posts and head (lintel) of the doorframe as a sign to avert the worst of the plagues, the death of the firstborn.

But Jesus is the "Lamb of God." His blood, first shed in the scourging, now flows from his thorn-crowned head. The blood of this lamb averts that most deadly of all blows: guilt and its companion, despair.

Christians for many centuries have been accustomed to think of the atoning death of Christ as something that took place only on the cross. But, to enter fully into the mysteries of the Passion, we have to take a more primitive view. Jesus met death and entered into contest (see pages 37–38) with death as soon as he was alone on the Mount of Olives. He was already dying, there in the Garden. The scourging and the thorns, too, were part of what killed him. So it is correct to compare the death of the original Passover lamb of the Hebrews, which happened during the night, with Jesus' own entry into death, which began on the Mount of Olives on Passover night.

Guilt is real, but it is perfectly needless for us to cower in despair before it. God declares that he has granted total amnesty on guilt, if only we will accept that amnesty. To reveal guilt's utter impotency to drag us to final defeat, Jesus put himself in the place of the lamb. Jesus is our Door. He even provides, from his own veins, the atoning blood that is splashed on the posts and head of that Door.

It is not that God requires the death of his beloved Jesus before he will put away the "anger" he feels for the human race. Jesus accepts death in the manner that God would wish us all to accept it: trusting in divine love. (Exodus 11–13)

D. The Way of the Cross [*Luke 23:26–32; Mark 15:21–22; Matthew 27:32–33; John 19:17*]

When Moses led the Hebrews from the Nile valley to the vicinity of the Red Sea, he was surrounded by thousands of people, but he was a very lonely man. To his rear, the armies of the Pharaoh pursued him, while the Hebrews milling around him had lost faith in his prophetic word. Seeing the waters ahead and the armies behind, they bitterly denounced Moses for the folly of having put them into that position.

How similar and yet how different was Jesus' walk through the streets of Jerusalem. Pilate, representing an imperial power as great as Pharaoh's, had handed him over to death. Jesus was pursued by the soldiers of Rome, who drove him through the streets. And many of the ordinary men and women crowding the streets that day denounced Jesus as bitterly as the Hebrews had denounced Moses.

Among the ancient peoples of biblical lands, death was often compared to a violent sea. Death overwhelms, drags, smothers, and drowns us in its darkest depths. Then, too, the Bible often compares the noise of a hostile crowd to the roaring of the sea. Jesus drew closer and closer to that awesome shore whence no one returns. Like Moses, he heard the roaring of the "waves" to his left and right and the taunts of the enemy behind. Few, if any, walked with him in faith. (Exodus 14)

E. The Death of Jesus [*Luke 23:33–56; Mark 15:22–30; Matthew 27: 33–61; John 19:17–42*]

Moses conquered the death-dealing waters through the power of God, who instructed him to extend his staff over the sea. Jesus, too, conquered the amassed forces of evil and death. But, when the stormy night had passed, instead of the bodies of drowned Egyptians strewn along the shores of death (Exodus 14:30), only one dead man was seen: Jesus himself! Here, indeed, was the death of the firstborn!

Jesus conquered death, not by turning it back on his enemies, but by coming to grips with it himself. He did not turn aside but went forward to the cross as he had been doing all his life. No one can demonstrate death's final inability to destroy us who is not willing to walk into the very land of death.

44. The Resurrection in Greater Depth

[*Luke 24:1–48; Mark 16; Matthew 28; John 20, 21*]

[For the Glorious Mysteries, see Appendix Two, page 162, columns two and three.]

The twisted smile of cynicism is abroad throughout the land. We have all struggled with our weaknesses, our neurotic tendencies, our foibles, our sins, to the point of being cynical about ourselves, and we are even clearer (naturally!) about other peoples' faults. When we are introduced to an apparently happy couple, we ask ourselves what their problem is. When someone appears to be unselfish, we wonder what's in it for him. We applaud ourselves for avoiding excessively high expectations in our human relationships, though this may mean merely that we are comfortable only with people whom we perceive as no better than we.

The problem with such thinking is that it is a distorted form of *baqqesh*. If we expect little, we will get little. We will come to think that a few decades of life, followed by eternal night, may be the only sensible outcome for people as disappointing as we.

All this changes when we are privileged to see into the inner nobility of any person. Still more does it change when we meet someone who is really peerless, as was Jesus. When Jesus died, his disciples did not merely mourn. They despaired. Here was someone who *ought* to have lived on into glory, but who had apparently died miserably, with all of his goals unrealized.

As we meditate on the mystery of the resurrection, our greatest joy is the simple fact that someone who deserved to have life on a higher plane actually found it. Cynicism is not our noblest state of mind, and we are glad when our thoughts are washed free of it. Then there is the further joy of knowing that the resurrection expected by Jesus, found by Jesus, and revealed by Jesus, is something that we, in our multitudes, may also find.

It seems wonderfully right that Jesus, the man whom many regard as having been raised, as having found the future of all human development, was one who had a clearly superior idea of resurrection (see pages 85–87). And in this Jesus had good teachers, for the rudimentary notion of resurrection, which Jesus enriched, came from the *hasidim,* an intensely spiritual circle in the Judaism of the last two centuries before Christ. These people longed to see a resurrection in which their immediate ancestors, who had suffered and died for the cause of God, would return to life. There was no cynicism here: the Jewish martyrs were considered unquestionably worthy of resuming their lives. For them, resurrection would not merely be something nice. It would be an act of justice!

To appreciate the resurrection, we must study the life and teachings of Jesus in order that we, too, may feel that his resurrection was an act of justice. Further, we must not close our eyes to the injustices suffered by our fellow human beings. We cannot really appreciate the value of the resurrected life unless we appreciate the loss, the injustice, suffered by humans who have had their potential for development cut off prematurely.

It is easy to say, as some presumably spiritual people do, that death is after all just what we deserve for our sins. Technically that may be so, but we can applaud the fact that God is never satisfied with plans that are merely technically correct! He sees, much better than we do, all our sufferings, all our lost potential, and he plans for their ultimate fulfillment.

Jesus went around his homeland searching out other people. He was never satisfied with a superficial acquaintance but sought out the real person, the person unknown even to himself. He celebrated the basic glory of human life as such, without its surface adornments of wealth or position or even the temporary blessings of youth and health. He spoke with urgency, knowing that the time for moral growth, for discovery, might well be short. When we praise Jesus "raised," we praise the man who understood the richness of human potential and the possible fulfillments that could be obtained in the state called resurrection.

None of us has experienced a resurrected person, so we would do well, in meditation, to avoid trying to picture one. We can rejoice with Mary that her son, *our* lord, is raised, even without knowing, directly, what that means. True joy is contagious. We can rejoice with someone who has passed the bar without having the slightest idea what torture four years at a law school can be. We can rejoice with a person who is enjoying a work of art, even if its value is lost on us. If our appreciation of resurrection is weak, at least we can rejoice with those who rejoice.

The first Glorious Mystery, then, should be approached with a spirit of rejoicing that Jesus, the deserving man, found his (and our) future. We share the joy of his mother and of his disciples, who knew his value firsthand. And we share the joy of all who have discovered him in prayer, scripture, or sacrament.

The resurrection is often dismissed as impossible and unworthy of acceptance by serious thinkers. Such critics often have fewer objections to the spiritual elements of resurrection than to its bodily aspects. Despite the materialism and pleasure seeking of our age, there is a simultaneous, but contrary drift toward a disrespect for the body. We see it, perhaps, in the rape of the environment and in attempts to hide or even eliminate the poor, the suffering, the very old, and the very young.

We explain that the resurrection is the fulfillment of human potential, an idea that nearly everyone finds attractive; but when we go on to point out that human potentials are always connected—in one way or another—to matter, many critics balk because they do not believe that a material being would be worth resurrecting. When we admit that our corporeal powers, in the resurrection, are lifted to such awesome and unforeseen heights as to seem almost the equivalents of spiritual or mental powers, these critics are less antagonized but still very doubtful.

And yet, as has been noted, many of those same skeptics, having delved into modern physics, are fans of science fiction and believe that time travel has probably already been achieved by advanced beings elsewhere in the universe. It was for such moderns that I pointed out (number 31) that the resurrection implies that Jesus found the future and conveyed this to his disciples.

If we define the future as the "place" where all fulfillments emerge, where all threads come together in a single knot, then it is further clear that, in such a "place," all time would be absorbed into a constant "now," all development having ceased. Yet that is no more than the traditional definition of eternity: the possession of all goals in a single "now." Time travel itself would be open to anyone in that future-now, since all elements of the past would then be gathered up in unity. And a person coming from that future into our now would certainly bring all his or her fulfillments at the same time. Such a person would appear almost as a spirit, so intense would these powers be. When critics say they cannot believe that dead bodies can live again, I can agree: the body that lives again is the summation of all its former moments, gathered into "nontime" or "eternal now." Jesus, in coming back from that eternity to first-century Jerusalem, brought a corporeality that was indeed his distinctive corporeality, not a mere resuscitation of that which had died.

No one in the actual act of saying the rosary can pause to ponder the implications of science or even of theology. But what one *can* do is be aware of the fact that, in this mystery, we praise God for giving "Thy Kingdom come" a richer meaning for us. We can rejoice in the overthrow of cynicism by the *justice* of Jesus' resurrection. Even if we cannot yet *see* the future and all its brilliant fulfillments, we can have the joy of reaching out and touching it. This perception will, of itself, help to speed our meditation along.

When we recall that God can do anything for which humans have a pure hope, we can see that the mystery of the resurrection, because it gives us hope of our own resurrection, is in a way the mystery that saves us. It is insufficient to think of the death of Jesus to get a full insight as to why he is our savior. The death and resurrection together constitute the paschal mystery, and it is the risen Lord as much as the dying Lord who saves.

We are not told that Jesus revealed the resurrection to Mary. Jesus, it seems, revealed the resurrection to those who had lost hope. If Mary had hope enough to permit the birth of a Messiah rooted in divine existence, then she also had resurrection-hope (pages 111–13), whatever her actual ideas on resurrection.

This is not to say that Mary did not grieve bitterly for the suffering and death of her son. But, unlike the disciples, she had never lost hope that somehow God would give Jesus a truly adequate vindication. Doubtless she recognized the new faith of the disciples as the beginning of Jesus' full victory. Had Mary not been capable of resurrection-hope all along, would she have provided adequate parenting to the Messiah?

As Mary watched the Church being born anew, by the power of the revelation of the man of the world to come, she must have relived the Annunciation. Here was promise of a new Church, a gathering of firstborns, needing now only to find confidence in herself as having been given a divine mission and the power to pursue it.

[Review also Appendix Three, pages 165–66, under "The Resurrection."]

45. The Ascension in Greater Depth

[*Luke 24:49–51; Acts 1:6–11; Mark 16:19, 20*]

The Ascension is really a two-sided mystery: it begins with the sinking realization that Jesus is now impossibly far away. He will not walk with us as before. But the other side of the mystery is that he is now available in many ways (prayer, Scripture, sacrament), actually reaching out to more people than he did in Judea and Galilee.[35]

When Jesus was among his disciples, they felt he was very near, yet they misunderstood him. In a sense he was very far. After his death, they assumed he was far, yet they came to understand him better, so that he was, in reality, very near. So too with us. When we seek the Father we seek Jesus with him (in the distance). But we have the daily experience of finding him to be very near.

Why is Jesus able to touch us now? Because he is exalted "to the Father's right hand," becoming our advocate, our mediator; because the Spirit of God flows forth as he directs; because the whole course of history is tending toward his ideals and will one day be delivered to him; because that day in the future already exists in eternity and Jesus is its Lord. He toward whom all tends was the pattern from which all things took their origin, hence the Divine Name "Lord" is not misappropriated when it is given to him.

---

[35] For a fuller discussion of the Ascension along these lines, see my book *From Bible to Creed*, op. cit., pages 124–31.

It is only through symbol that the far can be made near, not empty symbol, but the sort of full symbol such as the Divine Name that gives access to that which it symbolizes. Thus the Ascension is the mystery of the Divine Name as our meeting place with Jesus Christ. It is also the mystery of sacrament, in which we have access, under symbols sealed in the Name, to realities that remain beyond our ken.

At a time when we are seeking something we cannot see directly, a symbol gets us pointed in the right direction. It focuses our *baqqesh*. The nearer the approach of the thing we seek, the more it fills the symbol. When Jesus died, he became the Church's powerful symbol directing its search for God. So effective is Jesus in hastening the approach of God that the Church correctly said that he is actually the Divine Name, the most perfect symbol.

Because the Church understood its Ascended Lord better than it understood him while he yet breathed our air, the Church began to realize what its mission should be. The disciples, as we saw on page 99, then returned to Jerusalem for a period of *qawweh* in which they were to await being clothed in power from on high.

The Resurrection restored the Church's hope, and the Annunciation, also, had been a mystery of hope. Similarly the time of *qawweh* after the Ascension was a time of faith, much as the Visitation had celebrated faith. It is not surprising that Luke now (Acts 1:14) alerts us to Mary's presence in the midst of the Christian community; she had brought to the Annunciation and Visitation the very hope and faith that the Church was only now discovering. She had once carried an unseen Messiah.

[Review also Appendix Three, p. 166, under "The Ascension."]

46. The Descent of the Holy Spirit in Greater Depth

[*Acts 2:1–41*]

The Holy Spirit is, of course, the Spirit of God. The mystery of Pentecost is very much a mystery of Jesus, for it was Jesus who, in death, obtained for the world this new outpouring of the Spirit. (The Spirit, like the resurrection, is the coming of the future.) And it was not a Spirit with which Jesus had been unfamiliar! It was the same Spirit that he had breathed all his life. Moreover, the divine existence upon which Jesus' human existence rests had been in eternal communion with God Father and God Spirit.

In the Ascension, the disciples learned to think of Jesus as at the right hand of the Father, as their mediator. In this mystery, we see how wonderfully Jesus served to send them what they needed.

Acts 1:14 places Mary, as we have seen, with the Church in Jerusalem, and rosary tradition has always extended her presence to the nearby event of Pentecost. For purposes of meditation, this extension (which in any case is not unlikely) is illuminating, because the gifts that the Church needed from the Spirit of God for its mission were precisely the gifts that Mary had needed to be the mother of the Messiah. The Church would need to listen to the Word of God in faith as Mary had done. The Church would need to make intercession for others as Mary had done (John 2:3).[36] The Church would need to give birth to newness of life in its members; Mary had conceived of the Holy Spirit. The Church would need to lead the new Christian through many stages of instruction and nourishment; Mary had performed these services for the young Messiah himself. In short, the Church needed to be a mother in the style of Mary. *She needed to be Marianized.*

As we learn from the Annunciation, the only limit to God's blessings is that imposed by our lack of hope. But there was no hope like Mary's. We ought not to be surprised that the Church of Pentecost was so endowed and so vigorous that "three thousand were added that day" (Acts 2:41 [NAB]).

As Mary observed Pentecost and its fruits, she must have thought of the Annunciation and Nativity. Luke himself regards Pentecost as a sort of repetition of those earlier mysteries. It is he who describes for us how Mary was told in the Annunciation that

---

[36] John's purpose in the Cana story is clearly not to reveal Mary as an intercessor (see Pheme Perkins, "Mary in Johannine Tradition," in *Mary: Woman of Nazareth*, op. cit., page 113.) John's point, according to Perkins, is that Mary shows that "true intuition of faith" that characterizes authentic discipleship. This, however, is close enough to my own description of intercession (pages 16–17) to justify citing John 2:1–12 here. The Church herself could not do better than to approach God with a true intuition of faith.

"the Holy Spirit will come upon you" and the "power of the Most High will hover over you (Luke 1:35)," just as the Spirit came down and hovered over the assembly at Pentecost.

In this mystery we realize that we too need to be *Marianized*, we too need the gifts of the Spirit with which she was endowed and that her son breathed so naturally. Just as the early Church placed Mary in its midst, so do we when we ask her to "pray for us sinners now and at the hour of our death."

[Review also Appendix Three, pages 166–67, under "The Descent of the Holy Spirit."]

47. The Assumption in Greater Depth

In the Old Testament the term *assumption* (taking up) is used in connection with God's "taking" Israel from Egypt "up" on eagles' wings, to the safety of his mountain home in the Sinai wilderness (Exodus 19:4). In the same way, the New Testament speaks of the Church being taken on eagles' wings to a place of special protection in the wilderness (Revelation 12:6, 14). The Church is always in need of being "taken up" on God's protective wings while her journey on earth still lasts, and of being "taken up" definitively at the end of the world.

In this mystery (see page 100), Mary, the embodiment of the Church, has again already done that which the Church needs to do. She has already been taken up on the wings of God.

The ancient Israelites generally thought that deceased people are in their graves. Though they are sometimes aware of the words of graveside visitors and appreciate our attention, the dead are so limited that they are often said to be asleep. Yet the Israelites believed that some of the great people whose power they could clearly feel were actually *awake*. Some, in fact, were so awake as to have been assumed into the presence of God. Elijah's assumption is described in the Bible (2 Kings 2), while the assumptions of Moses and Isaiah and others are described only in extrabiblical writings. Against this background it is not surprising that the Church could eventually come to understand Mary as being awake and assumed.

In Jewish tradition, Moses, Elijah, and Isaiah (as well as others) were admitted to God's presence after death because they had already been admitted to it, at least occasionally, during life. The human being who accepts a mission from God becomes the special friend of God, over whom God extends his protective wings. The friend of God has already breathed the air of heaven, seen heavenly things, and lived. He or she has been transformed in some way, becoming a naturalized citizen of heaven who may look forward to assumption.

Moses, for example, had gone up Mount Sinai and met with God, and, as God's friend, conversed with God in the tent shrine that the wandering Israelites carried from site to site (Exodus 33:11; Numbers 12:7–8; Deuteronomy 34:10). Elijah, too, talked with God on Mount Sinai, and God sent ravens and angels to feed him in the wilderness (1 Kings 17:6; 19:1–18). In the writings of Hosea, the nation of Israel is God's bride; even after her national sins, God promises to protect her in the wilderness (Hosea 2:8–22). I have already mentioned that Israel (Exodus 19:4) and the early Church (Revelation 12:6, 14) were assumed, for their own protection, into the desert camp of God.

We may say that Mary has been assumed because she, the embodiment of the Church, had also stood in the divine presence in the Annunciation and during her life with the Eternal Word. (The Annunciation [see page 113] portrays Mary as a prophet so sublime that her journeys are her messages.) God protected her in her mission to show how he would protect all his people. In Mary the promise of protection has been realized to the full, just as in Mary, God's Annunciation (and the other mysteries) were also realized to the full.

Because in Hebrew thought a human being was not divided into body and soul, it was taken for granted that anyone who had been assumed must have been taken up as a whole person. It is not surprising that Jewish tradition has never pointed to the resting places of Moses, Elijah, or Isaiah.

Similarly, though both Ephesus and Jerusalem claim the tomb of Mary, neither claims her mortal remains. If she has been "taken up," she has been taken as a whole person. In the Catholic Church this idea has been preserved in cultures that *do* divide body from soul by an insistence that Mary has been assumed "body and soul." It must be remembered, however, that her corporeality is a corporeality of the future; there is little point in our imagining what sort of body is hers.

When we replace the ancient images of assumption with modern theology, we start with the idea that, by the mission and special graces that she had been given, Mary was able to pass along to Jesus, through his birth and training, a human nature full of the best virtues, instincts, disciplines, and feelings. Through such gifts as these, entrusted to her for the sake of Jesus and humanity, Mary's own fulfillment had been achieved in this life and would not be suspended in death.

I have mentioned the difference between the Resurrection of Jesus and the Assumption of Mary as consisting above all in this, that while Jesus revealed the Resurrection, Mary has no such honor or function. Although there have been many claimed apparitions of Mary in Christian history, no one has ever claimed to have seen the "risen Mary." Any apparition of hers will be something of a lesser order, perhaps less direct, something that would not lead anyone to suppose that Mary was "alive among us," for however short a time. As a matter of plain historical fact, not even the earliest ages of the Church ever claimed to have seen the risen Mary. The doctrine of her Assumption was not proclaimed by witnesses and was not even preached in the earliest centuries. The Assumption is a mystery that the Church attained through an internal process of reflection and deduction.[37]

Putting it another way, while the *baqqesh* of Jesus actually pierced through to the resurrected future, Mary's *baqqesh* pierced through to Jesus. Mary is not the conqueror, the victor, except

---

[37] All this is admitted by no less an authority than Joseph Cardinal Ratzinger (*Daughter Zion*, pages 72–82), prefect of the Congregation for the Doctrine of the Faith. Cardinal Ratzinger goes on (pages 79–81) to connect the Assumption to the ancient idea, visible already in Colossians 3:3 and Ephesians 2:6, that the Church itself is already "ascended."

insofar as she adheres to Christ, as all of us are called to do. Precisely because the fruits of redemption were available to her *in anticipation*, there can be no thought that she somehow obtained anything by herself.

It seems that God assumed Moses and Elijah not just because they accepted his mission and became his friends; they were also to be protected as witnesses who could appear to a future generation (Mark 9:1–8). Is the assumption of Mary related to the fact that she, too, has become a witness? The nature of Mary's ongoing witness is the subject of the final mystery of the rosary.

When we rejoice in the mystery of the Assumption, then, we rejoice in the protection that God extends to those who have stood in his presence and for whom he has some special ongoing or future purpose. It is a more passive concept than that of resurrection. For ourselves, we must understand that our eventual assumption will depend on our living, now, in his presence as much as we can.

[Review also Appendix Three, page 167, under "The Assumption."]

48. The Crowning of Mary as Queen in Greater Depth

Mary is called Queen because she is Intercessor, Listener (see page 101). She is, in glory, what the Church is, in tribulation: our Mother. And the testimony of the ages bears this out. The Church, even in the most fervent and best administered dioceses of the world, fails to reach some of us. This may be due to lack of dedication on the part of our neighbors. It may be due to the scarcity or the bad example of pastors. It may be because even the best of programs and legislation may not fit our case exactly. Most often it may be the simple fact that nothing run by human beings ever succeeds completely. For whatever reasons, even the most loyal of Christians sometimes find themselves with no one to minister to them. At such times, bruised and suffering people by the millions have moved closer to Mary, the first mother, and have found the powers of their souls blossoming under her influence.

If Mary has been assumed on eagles' wings to be a witness, to what does she testify? Clearly, she shows us what the Church should be. Jesus revealed the Father; Mary reveals the Church: giving birth, nurturing, loving, listening, interceding, sponsoring, educating, and exercising a mother's rule.

It is no accident that Mary, in the modern Church, is sponsor of the rosary. Based firmly on the act of greeting God, the rosary keeps us in the presence and protection of God, the very requirement that all must meet who seek their personal assumption.

[Review also Appendix Three, pages 167–68, under "The Crowning of Mary."]

6

The Rosary: Gateway to Contemplation

49. Contemplation

Contemplation, as I have described it in number 13, page 26, signifies "our openness to the activity that is *not* primarily ours, but comes from divine Reality itself." In this part of the book I evaluate that openness in ourselves.

Too often contemplation has been portrayed as something available only after meditation is mastered, a sort of higher level reserved for the special few. Some have even equated contemplation with mystical experiences: direct visions, as it were, of God—special favors indeed! But though "mystical" and "direct" experiences do come under the heading of contemplation, contemplation itself is a much wider thing, not at all reserved for a tiny minority.

Most (all?) people have experienced contemplation (reality taking over), even though few have meditated. I have known highly contemplative individuals who have never given any thought to meditation. (This is not to say that such persons have no need of meditation; meditation, in fact, would greatly enhance even their contemplative experiences.)

God is active, as we can learn from our own journals, but God can touch us more directly, even, than we are able to see in our recorded daily events. He can actively touch us "person to person." Our openness to this touch is, as I have said, our contemplation.

God's infinite energy cannot normally touch our intellects directly, because they are too tiny. (I say "normally," because God does, it is claimed, quite rarely flood someone's contemplative intellect with the light of his glory.) Since, then, his touch is not to be expected in our intellects, we can expect it only in our hearts (wills). He probes with love. Our response is not to look for something intellectual (a brilliant insight, for example), because anything of that sort which we could see would not be he. Our response, rather, is simply *to be* for him, with him.

This fits in with what I said about *baqqesh* ("seeking," cf. numbers 7, 15, 28, and 31). The seeker holds himself or herself in readiness, waiting, looking. The "looking" is even active, an effort to discern. But while the seeker looks for "events," for signs of the approaching future of God, he or she knows there is another sort of approach, which is neither insight nor meaningful events, and is still less a direct vision of God.

Discerning God's Active Presence

When we think we are touched by God's active presence, his probe of love, we take care to simply "be" for him. But, paradoxically, he does not even grant us absolute assurance that what we detect is really he. We are compelled, even in this place, to walk in trust and not in vision. Thus arises the importance of discernment.

God's contacts are, then, tentative. We note them in our journals beside those other signs of presence, the language of events. We should talk about them to others, especially with our spiritual director (if we are lucky enough to find one). More importantly, we simply remember and wait. Very likely we will gradually develop greater surety in these matters as our "database" increases. But it is not necessary that we should: we can love God increasingly even if we always have to ask, during the approach of his love, "Is that you?"

Spiritual writers caution us not to mistake good feelings for the touch of God. Such feelings may come from him but, perhaps more often, they will be generated by our own good spirits. They may at times be masks for forces that are not even harmonized with God. We must keep in mind that God is always present to us, whether or not we "know" or "feel" his presence.

To be identifiable as divine, God's touch must nudge us in directions that are consistent with faith, good doctrine, conscience (when rightly formed), and with what God is saying to us in events. (Again, the journal!) If friends, Church, science, and tradition see us walking off in false directions, then we may well be deceiving ourselves.

The Rosary as a Place of Contemplation

God's touch of love may occur during or after rosary. Indeed it may come *before* rosary, in which case it is related to the previous rosary. Bernard Basset has linked contemplation with the "prayer of simple regard" (see pages 101–17 of *Let's Start Praying Again*). The expression "prayer of simple regard" implies that we are quiet before God. But, paradoxically perhaps, this does not mean that we must periodically halt our rosary or wait until it is finished. We *may* stop the rosary, and this method works well for beginners. But it is our goal in rosary meditation to absorb all the words and mysteries so completely that we are silent and open (contemplating) even when reciting it, indeed, *because* of reciting it.

Perhaps the clearest instance of this occurs in the third section of the Hail Mary, when, by reaching for God while talking to Mary, we may experience a marvelous opening. (See pages 44–46.)

And there are more subtle openings to God. A personal reflection may make this clearer. For a long time I (correctly enough) regarded the rosary as praising God to Mary. But how was I supposed to be open to God when I was talking to Mary? (I had not yet recognized that I could do both, particularly in the third section of the Hail Mary.) This dilemma was overcome, very naturally, in the course of time. I was talking to Mary, but, very gently, she began to make me really listen to the implications of my own words. I said, in the Annunciation, that Jesus is worthy of all hope. But, at length, Mary seemed to be challenging me: did I really believe what I was saying in this and the other mysteries? If so, what was I willing to do about it? (It often happens that when we enthusiastically expound some idea to a friend, a slight smile on our friend's face will ask us whether we are really much open to the insight we so bravely defend with words.)

No sooner had I perceived Mary's questions than I realized it was really God who was questioning me. God had "inspired" me, and Mary had reflected that inspiration back upon myself. Thus, God was tangibly present to me.

We do not have to be at prayer to experience this. In the height of enthusiastic sharing between friends, just when we would suppose that our own ideas and our joy in friendship would block out any special sensitivity to God, suddenly we know that God or, specifically, Christ, is with us. It is the lesson of Emmaus (Luke 24:13–35).

There is a great deal of self-conscious posturing in all of us. Like persons hearing their own voices coming over a microphone while they speak, we are confused by the feedback. It is the other side of our most precious ability, the ability to be conscious, however indirectly, of ourselves, and thus to acquire a sense of responsibility. But a great amount of rosary meditation will generally be needed before the wounded side of self-consciousness can be healed. Then, gradually, we can be free to know that God and Christ are present in the smile of Mary. She willingly defers to God or, better, says firmly to us, "Now you too are Firstborn! Hear him!" In each mystery, then, I speak of Christ to Mary. She, however, reminds me that I am firstborn now, to whom my Father calls.

Is Your Rosary "Working"?

Anyone interested in prayer cannot fail to notice how the rosary improves the life of prayer. This is, in itself, a great achievement, but this book is really much more about meditation and contemplation than about prayer as such. Learning to meditate will, of course, improve one's prayer, but the main interest here can be articulated in the simple question: Has the rosary taught you to meditate?

Meditation, according to Capra (see page xv), ought to give us an approach to reality that is *organic, unitive,* and *intuitive.* With these qualities, we may be sure that our meditation will support the contemplative within us.

Organic is perhaps the most subtle of the three goals. Certainly rosary meditation embraces all reality and tries to contact it as a whole, organically. The "cry into the limitless unknown" asserts our kinship with all that is, while intercessory prayer puts interdependence into action. All created beings have this in common, that is, their being is dependent on the one source of being.

There is an infinite difference between Creator and created, yet the rosary meditator should gradually sense the two together. A feeling of "creatureliness" should arise, enabling the meditator to intuit, at one time, both the dependency and the independence of individual created beings (see number 28, on the experience of dependency in beings). There is a "sisterhood of being" between all things and their Creator, even while the Creator is perceived to enjoy a bottomless depth of being. As meditation will help you recognize the individuality of even the humblest being and of the persons you greet, so your improved awareness will include their radical contingency.

Is your meditation becoming *unitive*? First, meditation should unite your powers. These are the basic powers of knowing, willing, faith, hope, and love. They are also the more specific powers of memory, attentiveness, endurance, openness, listening, acceptance, and the like. But, second, there should also develop an increasing awareness of the unity-in-diversity that exists between all things and between oneself and other beings. The availability of persons long dead, for example, helps us to sense the relativity of space and time. The way in which hope influences events can give us a powerful sense of the indeterminateness of reality and of the power of unitive forces such as radiate from events of love.

Finally, meditation should restore and enhance our *intuitive* powers. The very presence of the beings to whom we direct our knowing and willing should begin to speak to us, to change us. Our awareness of dependency, as taught by the Our Father (see page 37), and of our poverty (see page 76) slowly empowers us to intuit being as created and uncreated. Our responses to reality should become truer, more reliable.

This number is short, because it can really be written only in each person's journal. What God says to each of his many first-borns is, thankfully, far beyond the prophetic ken of any mere writer of books. It is yet to be revealed what garlands are being woven by Father and children in that Garden of Roses whose paths lead east of Eden.

50. The Rosary in Relation to the Eucharist and the Liturgy of the Hours

Contemplation can be choked by a life that is not well integrated, whose parts are not deeply interrelated. The rosary, then, must not be disruptive of work, family life, or the great liturgies. There is not space in this book for an elaborate tracing of the relationships between the Eucharist, the Liturgy of the Hours, and the rosary; I will limit myself here to suggesting a few ways of dovetailing. The reader must experiment with these and other ways, entering the results in the journal.

A. The Eucharist

The Eucharist is many things. It is the memorial presence of Christ (and not less real for being a memorial), and it is communion in that presence. Because no one has thanked God as did Christ, the presence of Christ makes his memorial a *eucharist* (Greek: "thanksgiving").

Our method of integrating the Eucharist with the rosary will depend on whether we say one, or more than one, chaplet each day, and on whether we wish to say some rosary before and after the Eucharist, or only before, or only after. It depends too, of course, on whether we can actually attend the Eucharist on a given day, or can only join our thoughts with it from our position at home or other work place.

As we approach the Eucharist, from near or far, we want to be fortified by the God-centered virtues of faith, hope, and love. These, as we have seen, are called forth by the Annunciation, Visitation, and Nativity. *After* Eucharist, we wish to be properly thankful: gratitude is a theme of the Presentation and, in another way, of the Finding. The Presentation and Finding also touch on Jesus' mission: the person renewed by the Eucharist needs to think of his or her own mission. Thus, the Eucharist fits well between the Nativity and the Presentation (as long as we remember that the Eucharist is primary, and it is really the mysteries that "fit" themselves to it).

On the other hand, the Sorrowful Mysteries touch on the necessity of accepting the will of God and on the sacrifice of Christ that is memorialized (made present) in the Eucharist. The Sorrowful Mysteries go well *before* the Eucharist. The Glorious Mysteries speak to us of Pentecostal life, life in the risen Christ, and so may fit well *after* the Eucharist.

If it be desired to insert the Eucharist *into* the Sorrowful Mysteries, we may consider that the first three of these mysteries describe our sorrows, pains, and needs: things we bring to the Eucharist. The last two Sorrowful Mysteries focus more on our identification with Christ as he leads us out of the dark valley by the path of fidelity to God. Thus the Eucharist might be placed after the third and before the fourth mystery. But one would want to compensate somewhat by recalling that we also bring elements of the Joyful and Glorious Mysteries to the Eucharist.

B. The Liturgy of the Hours

The Second Vatican Council paid high tribute to the Liturgy of the Hours (formerly called the Divine Office) and stated that it should be restored to the people. Under recent popes, that liturgy has been revised to render it more accessible to all. (It was the laity who, in early Christianity, adapted this liturgy from the Jewish temple.)

The Liturgy of the Hours is the great praise or thanksgiving directed by the Church to God in continuation of the Eucharist. Because it is pegged to the different hours of the day, it consecrates and integrates all our time. There are seven liturgical hours, the understanding being that the term "hour" does not refer to periods of sixty minutes, but merely to the times when portions of this liturgy are begun. The seven hours are: Morning (around sunrise), Midmorning, Midday, Midafternoon, Evening (around sunset), Night (around bedtime), and Vigil (during the night). The hour called Vigil is noted for its continuous readings and is usually transferred to any convenient time during the day, when it is called Office of Readings instead of Vigil. The revised liturgy also encourages busy people to consider choosing only one of the three daytime hours (Midmorning, Midday, or Midafternoon).

The Liturgy of the Hours taps a strong source of energy in the human soul: the fact that the soul has different moods corresponding to different times of day. Because it is built on the Psalms, themselves fully attuned to the wide spectrum of human emotions, the total effect of the Liturgy of the Hours is to enable us to praise God from the depths of the state of our own souls, or to enter sympathetically into the moods of other humans whose present condition may be different from our own. The Liturgy of the Hours, then, resonates in a way denied to all other liturgies and meditative practices.

The Liturgy of the Hours has, and deserves, many devoted practitioners. It is safe to say that no one can obtain an integrated life of prayer, meditation, and contemplation unless he or she takes at least some notice of the hours. But my experience is that people often begin the Liturgy of the Hours in an unrealistic way. They rush out and buy large volumes that contain all, or nearly all, of this liturgy. Then, on the first day that they cannot do it all, they think they have failed for that day and give up until the morrow. Soon they are giving up on every day.

A better procedure would be the following. The main point of the Liturgy of the Hours is to *observe the hours,* by which we mean simply to commemorate the different times of day, whether or not one has the official texts handy. Then, slowly, one can add to one's observance of the hours by drawing from the official liturgy.

For example, people who say grace at meals, even silently, already observe three of the hours: Morning, Midday, and Evening. People who recite the Angelus do the same. And people who pray upon rising and retiring are automatically observing Morning and Night. A person who reads from the Bible or other appropriate authors is observing Vigil or Office of Readings, as the case may be. (If one cannot attend Eucharist, the readings from the Eucharist may be more appropriate for this hour than its own proper readings.) And, of course, a person who prays parts of the rosary at different times is also observing various hours.

The following remarks are offered as a very general guide, subject to many exceptions:

The Joyful Mysteries fit well in the morning because they speak to us of hopes, of beginnings, of missions.

The Sorrowful Mysteries fit well at midday or during the afternoon, for they recall the *toil* of Christ in his passion, and his determination to see the task through. These hours, moreover, correspond to the actual times of the Way of the Cross and the Death of Jesus.

The Glorious Mysteries speak of fulfillments and may well be appropriate at the end of the day.

But the end of the day makes us think of the opportunities for tomorrow (Joyful Mysteries), while the beginning of the day is full of sunlight and glory, making us think of the Glorious Mysteries. Thus I do not try to lay down ironclad rules.

I must also avoid giving the impression that the rosary can substitute for the Hours. They are two different sorts of things. I only mean to say here that the rosary, too, can help to consecrate time and draw on the different moods of the day. It should be a goal of any Christian *eventually* to obtain the texts of the official liturgies and use them. Only these texts allow us to pray in union with others around the world. Meanwhile, however, it remains true that the first step is to learn to *observe the times* and attune our souls to them, something that the rosary, or even grace at meals, can help us do.

C. Gradual Integration of the Liturgy of the Hours

Liturgical experts tell us that the principal Hours are Morning and Evening and that the principal prayer for these two is the Our Father (which is not prayed at any of the other Hours). A user of the rosary who wishes *gradually* to integrate the Liturgy of the Hours into his or her life might well begin or conclude the morning and evening segments of the rosary by standing attentively (the most solemn of liturgical postures) and praying the Our Father.

Again, liturgical scholars assure us that the next most important prayers of the Liturgy of the Hours (after the two Our Fathers) are the Gospel Canticles. I therefore list these below and suggest ways of integrating them with the rosary and other aspects of our day.

51. The Gospel Canticles

A. Zachary's Canticle [Benedictus, *Luke 1:68–79*]
[Appendix Four, page 169]

The Church from time immemorial (perhaps from the very day Zachary's Canticle was composed!) has assigned this Canticle to Morning Prayer. It should be recited (or, preferably, sung) standing, just before the Our Father of which I spoke immediately above.

Every Christian should have copies of the Gospel Canticles at hand, and the *Benedictus* is no exception. It is really a eucharistic prayer, since it is a prayer of thanksgiving for God's having visited his people, raising up a horn of salvation for us. The Hebrew and Aramaic words for "salvation" are nearly identical to the

Hebrew and Aramaic forms of the name "Jesus," so we can readily understand that the *Benedictus* was designed to help us thank God for Jesus.

The *Benedictus* is called the Canticle of Zachary since it is used in Luke's Gospel to express Zachary's joy over the birth of his and Elizabeth's son, John. But despite its connection to Elizabeth, it does not fit particularly well into the Visitation. The *Benedictus* speaks of gratitude for Jesus, a characteristic of the Presentation. As Simeon calls Jesus the "Light of the Gentiles," so the *Benedictus* calls him the rising sun or star. As the Presentation treats of Jesus' mission, so the *Benedictus* treats of the mission of John, but we must understand it really means, in a deeper sense, the mission of any Christian. Hence the *Benedictus* and its accompanying Lord's Prayer will fit well after the Presentation or, indeed, after the conclusion of the Joyful Mysteries, provided that the time of recitation is the morning. We must never divorce the Liturgy of the Hours from the actual hours for which it is designed.

If the Sorrowful or Glorious Mysteries are being recited in the morning, they too will provide ample material to help us recite the *Benedictus*. Because Zachary's Canticle is truly a eucharistic prayer, it integrates even better with the Eucharist than with the rosary. And this is another reason why it has been assigned to the morning, near the usual time of the Eucharist.

B. Mary's Canticle [Magnificat, *Luke 1:46–55*]
[Appendix Four, page 170]

This fine canticle is part of the story of the Visitation and fits well at the beginning or end of any meditation on the Visitation. Christians, however, have always sung the *Magnificat* at Evening Prayer, a time which may not coincide with most peoples' recitation of the Joyful Mysteries.

The *Magnificat* illustrates, in a wonderful way, the whole role of Mary in the Church. I have said right along that Mary is the forerunner of the Church. At the end of the *Magnificat*, God is praised for accepting "Israel his servant," where "servant" can also mean "child." Clearly we are dealing with a mother figure who rejoices that *all the people* (here called "Israel his servant") are God's people and her collective "child." This reminds us of how Mary moved from her concerns for her Messiah child to concerns for the rebirth of the Church as a whole. At the beginning of the *Magnificat*, Mary rejoices because God has looked with favor on the lowliness of his servant Mary. This means that Mary (or the Church, later on) has married above her station; she has, by virtue of her union with God, produced a child (or children) of which God can proudly admit parenthood.

These thoughts are certainly appropriate to the Mary of the Joyful Mysteries, especially the Visitation. But since the Joyful Mysteries are not so likely to be utilized at the time of Evening Prayer, it may be better to connect the *Magnificat* with the Glorious Mysteries. After the Ascension we see Mary praying in the midst of the Church. In the Descent of the Holy Spirit we see the Church "Marianized" and giving birth. In the Assumption and Crowning we see Mary as an Intercessor and Mother helping the Church where its work may falter and pointing to the day when the Church itself will be assumed. Mary rejoices in her role in the Glorious Mysteries just as much, and for the same reasons, as in the Joyful. But in the Glorious Mysteries the full effect of her relationship to Christ has been made clear. To quote the *Magnificat*, "All generations shall call me blessed."

The *Magnificat*, with its following Our Father, may well be recited after the Glorious Mysteries, provided these are recited in the Evening. Otherwise it will fit after whatever part of the rosary we happen to be saying. In any case, it will give us a reminder of the Joyful Mysteries, which, perhaps, came much earlier in our day.

C. **Simeon's Canticle** [Nunc Dimittis, *Luke 2:29–32*] [Appendix Four, page 170]

Simeon's Canticle fits the Presentation in every way. However, as the Church wisely assigns this canticle to Night Prayer, it will probably not be possible to recite it after the Presentation or after the Joyful Mysteries. Like the *Magnificat*, it is a powerful reminder of what we have considered earlier in the day.

As we recite the Canticles of Mary and Simeon late in the day, they gently prepare us for the following morning when we may consider them again in the Joyful Mysteries.

This section may be summarized as follows: the rosary and Liturgy of the Hours are two very different things, and one cannot be a substitute for the other. But one can recite the Canticle of Zachary and an Our Father in the morning, the Canticle of Mary and an Our Father in the evening (before or after supper), and the Canticle of Simeon (with no Our Father) at bedtime. By so doing, one will have absorbed the most essential parts of the Liturgy of the Hours. During the rosary, one will be touched by the nearest gospel Canticle one has recited, and, during the Liturgy of the Hours, one will be touched by the nearest mystery of the rosary. These thoughts will follow the general lines sketched in this chapter.

If one meditates through more than one chaplet each day, then the Joyful Mysteries fit best in the morning, the Sorrowful in the afternoon, and the Glorious in evening. But other arrangements also have advantages.

52. A Rosary Retreat: Living the Mysteries

This concept enables one to experience each mystery in a format longer than the rosary provides and with more time for applying them to one's own situation. The fuller integration of the mysteries and life, which is the goal of the retreat, will allow meditation to become more contemplative. Although a formal retreat could certainly be organized along the lines suggested below, the material is primarily designed for personal reflection under one's own guidance. Nothing more than the topics of reflection are given, one for each of the fifteen mysteries of the rosary. Few persons would attempt to meditate on all fifteen topics on a given day; rather one or more may be taken over successive days. Then each day's recitation of the rosary will reinforce the retreat meditations already completed.

1. Annunciation

In this reflection, try to hope for a better you, a new child of God. You already have some of this hope, and you can take that fact as an annunciation of the birth of your better self. Mary, too, has received an announcement of your approaching rebirth.

2. Visitation

Carry yourself in the faith that God will aid the new you to come to birth. Realize that, even at this early stage, you are a greater blessing to others. You are being reshaped in the image of Christ; resolve to "visit" others with this blessing.

3. Nativity

Celebrate your birth as a new child of God, born in the image of Christ. Understand that all classes and conditions of society should find something in your mission about which to rejoice. Try to reflect Christ so that others may love him in you.

4. Presentation

You are presented, redeemed, and commissioned. You have the commission to be the prophet of Christ to the world.

5. Finding

You who have been lost are now found to be about your Father's business. Resolve to seek his will carefully and carry it out faithfully, trusting in him.

6. Agony in the Garden

Prepare yourself to be tested. Can you sympathize with your fellow human beings so much that their trials become your own? Will you die to self and live for God and his mission?

7. The Scourging

Place yourself in solidarity with all who suffer physical pain and thereby bear your own pains in a more Christlike manner. Are you willing to accept the utter helplessness that great pain brings? Are you determined to help ease the pain of others, even to the extent of sharing it?

8. The Crowning with Thorns

Place yourself in solidarity with all who are mocked, cursed, held in contempt. Christ paid the price of his own blood to achieve this sort of solidarity with others; what are you willing to pay?

9. The Way of the Cross

Will you love all your enemies, taking on yourself the death (suffering, and so forth) that you suspect your enemies have earned? Will you walk with those who walk alone?

10. The Death of Jesus

Place yourself in solidarity with all of those now dying and with the dying Christ. Be willing not only that you should die, but that all of you that is not of God should likewise die. Reflect that you are dead. But recall also the greater glory and service that you are rendering to God.

11. The Resurrection

Consider ways in which you can even now show forth the resurrected life. Can you show more of peace, joy, detachment, witness, the evangelical counsels, fidelity, praise? Can you become more meditative, loving? Can you develop your own potential, or at least cease creating obstacles to that development?

12. Ascension

Think how you can live the life of an ascended person, that is, how you can better intercede for others. How can you show others that Christ, though gone, is still close?

13. Descent of the Holy Spirit

How can you better share with others the gifts of the Holy Spirit? What qualities of Mary can you, with God's help, live and show forth? Can you trust in God more completely?

14. Assumption

The more you are awake to God, the more you will be awake to God's people, both now and after your death. What resolutions can you form?

15. Crowning

Speak to Mary about your use of the rosary. Ask, through her intercession, to be shown more of the rosary and to be given the courage to use it better.

Appendixes

Appendix One: The Apostles' Creed

I believe in God, the Father Almighty,
Creator of heaven and earth.

And in Jesus Christ, his only Son, Our Lord,
who was conceived by the Holy Spirit,
born of the Virgin Mary,
suffered under Pontius Pilate,
was crucified, died, and was buried.

He descended into hell.
The third day he rose again from the dead.
He ascended into heaven,
sits at the right hand of God, the Father Almighty;
From thence he shall come to judge the living and the dead.

I believe in the Holy Spirit,
the Holy Catholic Church,
the communion of saints,
the forgiveness of sins,
the resurrection of the body,
and life everlasting. Amen.

Appendix Two: The Prompters for the Mysteries

The Easiest to Remember (pages 102, 103)	*The Easiest to Use (pages 102, 103)*	*Baqqesh Series (page 103)*
1. in the Annunciation	announced	sought by Mary
2. in the Visitation	carried (borne) to Elizabeth	sought by Elizabeth
3. in the Nativity	born	sought by shepherds
4. in the Presentation	presented to God	sought by Simeon
5. in the Finding	found [about his Father's business]	sought by Mary and Joseph
1. in the Agony in the Garden	agonizing	seeking the Father's will
2. in the Scourging	scourged	seeking the Father's kingdom
3. in the Crowning with Thorns	crowned	seeking the Father's redemption
4. in the Way of the Cross	driven along the Way	seeking the Father's way
5. in Dying on the Cross	crucified	seeking the Father's glory
1. in the Resurrection	raised	sought/found among the living
2. in the Ascension	ascended [or "exalted"]	sought/found with the Father
3. in the Descent of the Holy Spirit	sending the Spirit	sought/found in the Spirit
4. in the Assumption	taking Mary up	sought/found by Mary
5. in the Crowning of Mary	crowning Mary	sought/found by the Church or by the Rosary

In Greater Depth (I) (pages 109–41)	*In Greater Depth (II) (pages 122–23, 125–29, 130–41)*	*Another Series (partly from page 124)*
1. given to the hopeful	Joy of Mary, joy of the Father	begotten of God
2. carried by the trusting	Joy of Elizabeth	welcomed by God's servants
3. welcomed by the loving	Joy of the whole people	laid in a manger
4. acknowledged by the grateful	Joy of all nations	a sign of contradiction
5. admired by the wise	Joy of the Father	lost to the Church
1. uncomforted by friends	accepting the sorrows of the people	sorrowing with all people
2. unpitied by his executioners	accepting the plagues (blows)	scourged with the downtrodden
3. mocked by the soldiers	our doorway and our lamb	mocked with the weak
4. displayed in the streets	alone in deadly waters	burdened as one of the enslaved
5. abandoned to death	dying for his pursuers	killed with the innocent
1. vindicated by God	returned from the future	Lord of all fulfillments
2. awaited by the Church	Mediator for the Church	Lord of our Now
3. worshipped in the Spirit	Marianizer of the Church	Lord of our Mission
4. joined by Mary/Church	Awakener of Mary/Church	Lord of our Church
5. served by Mary	Glory of Mary	Lord of prayer

Appendix Three: Let the Our Father Be Your Guide

[*The following are meant only as examples; they are not meant to replace insights that will come to the meditator in meditation.*]

ANNUNCIATION

Our Father who art in heaven	The Father is the ultimate source of all annunciations.
Hallowed be thy Name	Mary's hope is answered by an incarnation of the Name.
Thy Kingdom come	The Israel of Mary's time longed for the Kingdom. Jesus, Son of David, is heir to the Kingdom.
Thy will be done	Mary said, "Be it done unto me according to thy word."
Forgive us our trespasses	The Israel of Mary's day longed for peace and reconciliation with God.
Lead us not into temptation	The Kingdom cannot come without a struggle, a trial.

VISITATION

Our Father who art in heaven	*Father* is a term of trust, and the Visitation is the mystery of faith. "Visiting" is something God does, as when he comes to save or to reprove. Human visitations, like Mary's, should bring God's visit to others.
Thy Kingdom come	Where the visitor goes, there the Kingdom also goes.
Thy will be done	God visits to make his will known.
Forgive us	God visits to reconcile people with himself and with each other.
Deliver us from evil	God visits to deliver.

NATIVITY

Our Father who art in heaven	The child born in Bethlehem is God's unique Son.
Hallowed be thy Name	Jesus is the Divine Name made flesh. His birth night is holy.
Thy Kingdom come	Israel prayed for the Kingdom and it got its King.
Thy will be done	"Peace on earth, [God's] good will to men."
Give us this day our daily bread	"Bethlehem" means "Temple of Bread." Jesus is the Bread from God.
Forgive us . . . as we forgive	Forgiveness on earth is peace on earth.
Lead us not into temptation	At the peaceful crib, opposition seems far away.

PRESENTATION

Our Father who art in heaven	God is the Father of Jesus and, here, God claims his Son, returning him to Mary and Joseph only after stating what his service will be.
Hallowed be thy Name	The temple was built for the hallowing of God's Name. The temple itself is hallowed by Jesus' arrival there.
Thy Kingdom come	Simeon announced that the Kingdom will embrace all nations. Jesus is "Light of the Gentiles."
Thy will be done	In the Presentation, God reveals his will.
Forgive us	The Presentation of the firstborn obtains reconciliation.
Lead us not into temptation, but deliver us from evil.	"This child shall be for the rise and for the fall of many in Israel."

[*Continued, next page*]

THE FINDING IN THE TEMPLE

Our Father who art in heaven	"I must be about my Father's business."
Hallowed be thy Name	The Temple is the place where the Name is hallowed.
Thy Kingdom come	God's "business" is the Kingdom.
Thy will be done	Jesus must be about his Father's business (will).
Forgive us . . . as we forgive	Reconciliation is the Father's business

THE AGONY IN THE GARDEN

Our Father who art in heaven	Jesus often went before his Father at night to receive instructions concerning the Kingdom. The Agony is the last and most important of such communications.
Hallowed be thy Name	The mountain (Olivet) where Jesus meets the Father is holy ground, as was Mt. Sinai, where Moses heard God's Name.
Thy Kingdom come	Jesus has his attention fixed firmly on the coming Kingdom. He desires it so much that he will accept all sorrows to see it fulfilled.
Thy will be done	This is Jesus' principal prayer during the Agony.
Give us this day our daily bread	Even as death approaches, Jesus is concerned with our needs.
Lead us not into temptation	Jesus is now in the very mouth of the great struggle (temptation). "Father, if it be thy will let this cup pass me by." The disciples sleep, though Jesus asks them to pray that they too not enter the great trial.

THE SCOURGING, CROWNING WITH THORNS, THE WAY OF THE CROSS

Our Father who art in heaven	During suffering, Jesus keeps his attention on the Father.
Hallowed be thy Name	In the midst of suffering, Jesus continues to bless the Name of the Lord.
Thy Kingdom come	Jesus' acceptance of suffering gives the greatest possible glory to the Father and to his Kingdom.
Thy will be done	This remains Jesus' main thought during the Passion.

THE DEATH OF JESUS

Our Father who art in heaven	In death (total dependence) Jesus has nothing but the Father. Yet he can also experience the absence of God.
Thy Kingdom come	The moment of death is the moment of Jesus' exaltation in the Kingdom.
Thy will be done	Now Jesus has finished a life of perfect fidelity to the will of God.
Give us this day our daily bread	In giving himself, Jesus becomes our bread.
Forgive us . . . as we forgive	Jesus dies forgiving his enemies; his death is a reconciliation.

THE RESURRECTION

Our Father who art in heaven	It is the Father who vindicates Jesus by raising him.
Thy Kingdom come	The resurrection of Jesus teaches us that the Kingdom is a resurrection kingdom (a fulfillment of all human potential).
Thy will be done	We pray for the speedy completion of the Kingdom, even though this demands that we conform our wills to God's.

[*Continued, next page*]

Give us this day our daily bread	We try to live as already part of the resurrected life: we pray only for sufficiency in this world.
Forgive us . . . as we forgive	The risen Christ gave us a ministry of reconciliation.
Lead us not into temptation	We know that the day of general resurrection will be a rebuke to all evil, including our own.

THE ASCENSION

Our Father who art in heaven.	Jesus has ascended to the Father.
Hallowed be the Name	God has bestowed his holy Name on Jesus, exalting him to the right hand of his majesty.
Thy Kingdom come, thy will be done.	Through the intercession (mediation) of Jesus, the divine Kingdom and Will may be more fully realized.
Forgive us . . . as we forgive	Jesus mediates for our forgiveness. As he is no longer visibly present, we must extend his ministry of reconciliation.
Lead us not into temptation	Jesus will return from his place at the Father's right hand. His return will coincide with the climactic struggle.

THE DESCENT OF THE HOLY SPIRIT

Our Father who art in heaven	The Holy Spirit is the Gift of the Father.
Hallowed be thy Name	The Holy Spirit, like the Son, is the Divine Name and is to be hallowed (treated as holy).
Thy Kingdom come	The Holy Spirit enlivens the Kingdom. The Spirit endowsMary with the gifts of the Kingdom. Jesus sent the Spirit, thus Marianizing the Church.
Thy will be done	The Holy Spirit teaches the Will of God.

Give us this day our daily bread	Pentecost is Israel's feast of new bread. In Christ we are a new wheat enlivened by the Holy Spirit.
Forgive us . . . as we forgive	Jesus imparts his Spirit to be the soul of the ministry of reconciliation.
Lead us not into temptation	Pentecost is a day of fire and wind. For those who trifle with the Holy Spirit, the experience of God can be one of judgment.

THE ASSUMPTION

Our Father who art in heaven	Mary has been "taken" (assumed) to be with God.
Thy Kingdom come	All humanity is offered the gift of assumption.
Thy will be done	Mary is assumed because she "heard the Word of God and kept it." Assumption is also God's good will for us, but we too must hear and accept God's will on earth as it is heard and accepted in heaven. We must, like Mary, become Listeners and Doers of the Word.
Give us this day our daily bread	The Assumed One does not lose her concern for humanity's daily needs.
Forgive us . . . as we forgive	Mary is fully the Awakened One, because she has received the full effects of humanity's reconciliation with God.
Lead us not into temptation, but deliver us from evil.	To be assumed is to be taken to God, the safe refuge from all evil.

THE CROWNING OF MARY

Our Father who art in heaven	Mary's destiny, like the destinies of each of us, begins in the eternal word of the Father. As our Listener and Sponsor, Mary's sublime task is to pray the Our Father with us, helping us to become new children of God.

[*Continued, next page*]

Hallowed be thy Name	The children of God bear his Name and are called holy (saints) in that sense. Mary is Queen of Saints.
Thy Kingdom come, thy will be done.	Mary is Listener, Intercessor. Her chief concern in our regard is the building up of the Kingdom, and the furtherance of the will of God.
Give us this day our daily bread	Mary's own prayers are continuous and extend to all our needs.
Forgive us . . . as we forgive	Mary prays for the extension of God's redemptive will, the ministry of reconciliation.
Lead us not into temptation, but deliver us from evil.	Mary constantly prays to enlarge the number who are alert and watching for the last day.

Appendix Four: The Texts of the Gospel Canticles[38]

Canticle of Zachary [*Luke 1:68–79, see pages 152–53*]

Blessed be the Lord, the God of Israel;
he has come to his people and set them free.
He has raised up for us a mighty savior,
born of the house of his servant David.
Through his holy prophets he promised of old
that he would save us from our enemies,
from the hands of all who hate us.
He promised to show mercy to our fathers
and to remember his holy covenant.
This was the oath he swore to our father Abraham:
to set us free from the hands of our enemies,
holy and righteous in his sight
all the days of our life.

[*The following section is the prophetic commissioning of John the Baptist, but serves as the commissioning of each of us.*]

You, my child, shall be called the prophet of the most high;
for you will go before the Lord to prepare his way,
to give his people knowledge of salvation
by the forgiveness of their sins.
In the tender compassion of our God
the dawn from on high shall break upon us,
to shine on those who dwell in darkness and the shadow of death,
and to guide our feet into the way of peace. [Doxology]

---

[38] From *The Liturgy of the Hours,* trans. International Consultation on English Texts (New York: Catholic Book Publishing Company, 1975).

Canticle of Mary [*Luke 1:46–55, see pages 153–54*]

My soul proclaims the greatness of the Lord,
  my spirit rejoices in God my Savior
  for he has looked with favor on his lowly servant.
From this day all generations shall call me blessed:
  the Almighty has done great things for me,
  and holy is his Name.
He has mercy on those who fear him
  in every generation.
He has shown the strength of his arm,
  he has scattered the proud in their conceit.
He has cast down the mighty from their thrones,
  and has lifted up the lowly.
He has filled the hungry with good things,
  and the rich he has sent away empty.
He has come to the help of his servant Israel
  for he has remembered his promise of mercy,
the promise he made to our fathers,
  to Abraham and his children for ever. [Doxology]

Canticle of Simeon [*Luke 2:29–32, see pages 154–55*]

Lord, now you let your servant go in peace;
  your word has been fulfilled:
my own eyes have seen the salvation
  which you have prepared in the sight of every people:
a light to reveal you to the nations
  and the glory of your people Israel. [Doxology]

Further Readings

Basset, Bernard. *Let's Start Praying Again*. Garden City, N.Y.: Doubleday/Image, 1973.

Bloom, Anthony. *Beginning to Pray*. New York: Paulist Press, 1982.

Brown, Raymond. *The Birth of the Messiah: A Commentary on the Infancy Narratives of Matthew and Luke*. Garden City, N.Y.: Doubleday/Image, 1979.

Bryan, David. *From Bible to Creed*. Wilmington, Del.: Michael Glazier, 1988; distributed by Liturgical Press, Collegeville, Minn.

Capra, Fritjof. *The Tao of Physics*. Revised ed., New York: Bantam Books, 1984.

Carmody, Denise L., and John T. Carmody. *Eastern Ways to the Center: An Introduction to Asian Religions*. Belmont, Calif.: Wadsworth, 1983.

__________. *Western Ways to the Center: An Introduction to Religions of the West*. Belmont, Calif.: Wadsworth, 1983.

Catoir, John. *Enjoy the Lord: A Path to Contemplation*. New York: The Christophers, 1978.

Dollen, Charles. *My Rosary: Its Power and Mystery. A Book of Readings*. New York: Alba House, 1988.

Donnelly, Doris, ed. *Mary, Woman of Nazareth: Biblical and Theological Perspectives*. New York: Paulist Press, 1989.

Doohan, Leonard. *Luke: The Perennial Spirituality*. Santa Fe, N.Mex.: Bear & Co., 1985.

Gribbin, John. *In Search of Schrödinger's Cat: Quantum Physics and Reality*. London: Bantam Books, 1984.

Häring, Bernard. *Prayer: The Integration of Faith and Life*. Notre Dame, Ind.: Fides Publishing, 1975.

Harrington, Wilfrid J. *The Rosary: A Gospel Prayer.* New York: Alba House, 1975.

Link, Mark. *You: Prayer for Beginners and Those Who Have Forgotten How.* Niles, Ill.: Argus Communications, 1976.

Maloney, George A. *Alone with the Alone.* Notre Dame, Ind.: Ave Maria Press, 1982.

Merton, Thomas. *Zen and the Birds of Appetite.* Gethsemane, Ky.: Abbey of Gethsemane, 1968.

Metz, Johann B., and Karl Rahner. *The Courage to Pray.* New York: Crossroad, 1981. Originally published as *Ermutigung zum Gebet* (Freiburg im Breisgau: Verlag Herder, 1977).

O'Carroll, Michael. *Theotokos: A Theological Encyclopedia of the Blessed Virgin Mary.* Wilmington, Del.: Michael Glazier, 1982.

Panikkar, Raimundo. *The Trinity and the Religious Experience of Man.* New York: Orbis Books, 1973.

Perkins, Pheme. *Reading the New Testament.* 2d Edition. Mahwah, N.J.: Paulist Press, 1988.

Rahner, Karl. *The Trinity.* New York: Herder and Herder, 1969.

Ratzinger, Joseph Cardinal. *Daughter Zion.* San Francisco: Ignatius Press, 1983. Originally published as *Die Tochter Zion* (Einsiedeln: Johannes Verlag, 1977).

Sekida, Katsuki. *Zen Training: Methods and Philosophy.* New York: Weatherhill, 1975.

Simons, George F. *Keeping Your Personal Journal.* New York: Paulist Press, 1978.

Smith, Margaret. *The Way of the Mystics: The Early Christian Mystics and the Rise of the Sufis.* Oxford: Oxford University Press, 1978.

Walsh, James, ed. *The Cloud of Unknowing.* Ramsey, N.J.: Paulist Press, 1981

Wiesel, Elie. *Souls on Fire: Portraits and Legends of Hasidic Masters.* New York: Random House/Vintage, 1972.

Index of Biblical Quotations

General Index